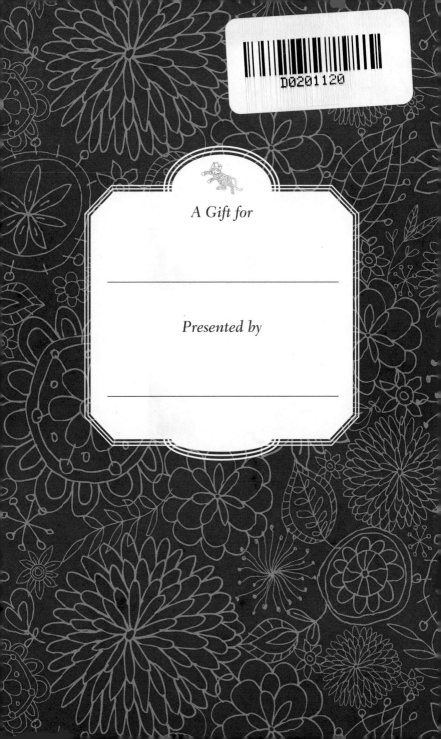

A Gift for

_____

Presented by

_____

Spilling
the Beans
on the Cat's
Pajamas

Spilling
the Beans
on the Cat's
Pajamas

Popular Expressions—What They
Mean and How We Got Them

JUDY PARKINSON

The Reader's Digest Association, Inc.
New York, NY/Montreal

A READER'S DIGEST BOOK

First published in Great Britain in 2009 by Michael O'Mara Books Limited
9 Lion Yard
Tremadoc Road
London SW4 7NQ

READER'S DIGEST TRADE PUBLISHING
U.S. Project Editor: Siobhan Sullivan
Canadian Project Manager: Pamela Johnson
Canadian Project Editor: Jesse Corbeil
Project Production Coordinator: Nick Anderson
Senior Art Director: George McKeon
Executive Editor, Trade Publishing: Dolores York
Associate Publisher: Rosanne McManus
President and Publisher, Trade Publishing: Harold Clarke

Library of Congress Cataloging-in-Publication Data
Parkinson, Judy.
 Spilling the beans on the cat's pajamas : popular expressions? What they mean and
how we got them / Judy Parkinson.
    p. cm.
"A Reader's Digest book."
ISBN 978-1-60652-171-7
1. English language--Idioms--Dictionaries. 2. English language--Terms and phrases.
3. Figures of speech--Dictionaries. I. Title.
PE1689.P296 2010
423'.13--dc22
                          2010016226

"Old expressions are the best, and short ones even better."

–Winston Churchill

INTRODUCTION

The English language has flourished over the centuries. Our ever-flexible language often revives phrases that we thought had "bitten the dust"—and new words and expressions creep into the lexicon all the time. There's a different "flavor of the month" for each generation.

So "strike while the iron's hot": If you want "to bone up" on the origins of some of the curiosities of the English language, look through these pages and you'll be "in seventh heaven." This book is "the cat's whiskers" and "the cat's pajamas," all rolled into one, as it "spills the beans" on the origins of all these expressions and many more.

I will "make no bones" about it, and I won't "beat around the bush" (after all, don't forget I'm "talking turkey" here): This book contains some fascinating and remarkable stories about our best-loved and most colorful phrases. The staples of our language—those familiar, well-worn expressions and clichés—originate from the most diverse sources. From main street to Homer, from advertising to social networking websites, from the army to the air force, from stage to screen…it's an "all-singing, all-dancing," around-the-world trip through our language's history.

If you've ever gone "over the top," you can thank the military. "Walk the plank" and "shake a leg" are both nautical terms, and I wouldn't be "rubbing salt in the wound" to say that that's another one. The world of sport, meanwhile, provides rich pickings. "To throw in the sponge" and "to come up to scratch" are both boxing terms, and baseball has allowed us "to take a rain check." But that's for another time. Look no further; you'll be "as pleased as Punch."

⁊ A ⳾

ADD INSULT TO INJURY

To hurt, by word or deed, someone who has already suffered an act of violence or injustice. The expression has been in use for centuries.

During the Augustan era, the so-called Golden Age of Latin literature, Phaedrus translated Aesop's fables into Latin verse, peppering them with anecdotes of his own. He quotes the fable about a bald man who tried to swat a fly that had bitten him on the head, but who missed the insect and instead slapped himself hard on the head.

Seeing this the fly then remarked, "You wished to kill me for a mere touch. What will you do to yourself since you have added insult to injury?"

ALIVE AND KICKING

Active and in good health. The expression was coined in the late eighteenth century and probably referred originally to a healthy baby, either while still in the womb or just after birth.

ALL CATS LOVE FISH, BUT FEAR TO WET THEIR PAWS

A traditional saying, dating back to at least the sixteenth century, used to describe a person who is eager to obtain something of value, but who is not bold enough to make the necessary effort or to take the risk.

It is to this saying that William Shakespeare referred in Macbeth (1:7):

Letting "I dare not" wait upon "I would,"
Like the poor cat i' the adage.

ALL IN A DAY'S WORK

Said of an unusual or unexpected task that can be obligingly included in the normal daily routine.

The expression was common by the eighteenth century and may stem from the nautical use of the term "day's work," which referred to the reckoning of a ship's course during the twenty-four-hour period from noon one day to noon the next.

A character in Sir Walter Scott's novel *The Monastery* says, "That will cost me a farther ride...but it is all in the day's work."

ALL OVER BUT THE SHOUTING

This expression is firmly rooted in the world of sports and was first used in print by nineteenth-century sportswriter Charles James Apperley in 1842. It means that victory is in the bag, only the cheering of the crowd at the end of the game or contest remains to come.

The phrase may perhaps be derived specifically from boxing—the shouting being the noisy appeal from the supporters of one of the boxers against the referee's decision.

It is also often applied to political elections in which the outcome is certain, even before the ballot papers have been counted.

ALL SINGING, ALL DANCING

This piece of popular phraseology was inspired by the first Hollywood musical, *Broadway Melody*, in 1929—the era in which sound first came to the movies, which was advertised with posters proclaiming:

The New Wonder of the Screen!
ALL TALKING
ALL SINGING
ALL DANCING
Dramatic Sensation!

The phrase caught on immediately, and two rival studios used the same sales pitch in the same year for *Broadway Babes* and *Rio Rita*.

In about 1970, the computing world adopted the phrase to hype up new software, so that by the mid 1980s, every kind of organization seemed to boast that their computers and systems packages had some quality that was "all singing, all dancing."

Subsequently, the expression has been linked with anything from savings plans, pensions and mortgages to machines—especially electronically controlled machines—of almost any kind.

A saying with a similar meaning is the older phrase "All the bells and whistles," which also describes that all-important "wow" factor.

ALL TARRED WITH THE SAME BRUSH

Everyone in the group shares the same failings; they're all sheep of the same flock. This old saying alludes to the methods used by farmers to mark their sheep. A brush dipped in tar was applied to the wool as a form of branding.

The phrase is now often used when people feel they have been lumped in with others and judged unfairly as a result.

ALL THAT GLITTERS IS NOT GOLD

Appearances are not what they seem. A saying that must have been in use for a thousand years or more and a favorite of poets, it is thought to be Latin in origin. It is a well-known note of prudence in Shakespeare's *The Merchant of Venice* (2:7):

> All that glisters is not gold,
> Often have you heard that told.

This implies that the proverb dates from earlier wisdom; certainly it was used by Geoffrey Chaucer in *The Canterbury Tales*, for in "The Canon's Yeoman's Tale," he wrote:

> However, all that glitters is not gold,
> And that's the truth as we're often told.

Many other writers have referenced it, including Thomas Gray in his "Ode on the Death of a Favourite Cat, Drowned in a Tub of Gold Fishes," but perhaps the most cynical use is that of Ogden Nash, who observed in "Look What You Did, Christopher":

> All that glitters is sold as gold.

ANNUS HORRIBILIS

A particularly bad or miserable year, the phrase being Latin for "horrible year." It owes its popularity to Queen Elizabeth II, who used it in a speech at a banquet in the Guild Hall, London, in 1992—the year that saw the divorce of the Princess Royal, the separations of the Prince and Princess of Wales and of the Duke and Duchess of York, and the devastating fire at Windsor Castle.

The next day, the punning headline writers **had a field day** (see page 77), with *The Sun* proclaiming on the front page, "One's Bum Year."

"Annus horribilis" was a play on a phrase with the opposite meaning—annus mirabilis, which was first used as the title of a poem by John Dryden to describe the year 1666, which he saw as an example of miraculous intervention by God.

It has ever since been used to describe particular years full of wonders or achievements; 1759 was one such for the British, in which they achieved a string of military successes (in British naval history, 1759 is also known as the "Year of Victories").

ANOTHER NAIL IN THE COFFIN

A depressing phrase that is applied to a development that makes a situation progressively worse. It refers to something that accelerates the failure of something or someone. The final nail can be compared with the "last straw" (see **clutching at straws,** page 49).

The phrase "another nail in the coffin" was also adopted by smokers. As early as the 1920s, they referred to cigarettes as "coffin nails," and this expression became the stock response whenever someone accepted yet another cigarette.

At the time, they were referring to the hazards of a smoker's cough; the links between smoking, cancer and heart disease were only recognized later (when cigarettes earned another nickname—"cancer sticks").

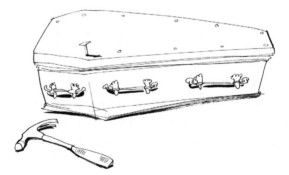

ANTS IN ONE'S PANTS

Said of an excessively restless or over-eager person.

The expression was popularized by Hugh S. Johnson, a dynamic former U.S. Army general who was in charge of the National Recovery Administration (NRA) in 1933–34, when the national reconstruction policies of President Franklin D. Roosevelt's "New Deal" were implemented.

He said of the NRA general counsel Donald Richberg: "Donald's agitation is just a symptom of the ants of conscience in his pants."

THE APPLE OF ONE'S EYE

"The apple of one's eye" is what one cherishes most. The pupil of the eye has long been referred to as the "apple" because it is perfectly round and was originally thought to be solid.

Because sight is so precious, someone who was called this as an endearment was similarly precious, with the result that the phrase took on the figurative sense we still retain.

The Bible employs the phrase many times, including:

> Keep me as the apple of the eye, hide me under the shadow of thy wings.
>
> Psalms 17:8

Examples of the saying's use can also be found in the works of King Alfred, dating from the end of the ninth century.

Our modern word for the physical "apple of one's eye," "pupil," comes from Latin and appeared in English in the sixteenth century. It is figurative in origin; the late Latin original was pupilla, "little doll."

The word might have been applied to the dark central portion of the eye within the iris because of the tiny doll-like image of oneself that can be seen when looking into another person's eye.

AROUND ONE'S EARS

This colloquialism means to be in a very troublesome situation. It is a shortened form of the saying "to bring a hornets' nest down around one's ears." Similarly, "down around your ears" is often used.

The expression "to stir up a hornets' nest" implies the same degree of trouble as the phrase above—and suggests perhaps deliberate provocation, too.

ASK SOMETHING POINT BLANK

To ask a direct question. This is a sixteenth-century phrase from the sport of archery. The targets had a white (blanc in French) central spot, so the arrows were pointed at the white; that is, point blanc.

In military and artillery usage, "point blank" is a range at which there is no fall of shot due to gravity—in other words, a very close range. (Any projectile from a firearm "drops" from the point of aim as the range increases, which in turn means that the farther the target, the higher the weapon has to be aimed above it.)

❧ B ❧

BACK TO SQUARE ONE

To begin again, or, less formally, "Back to where you started, sunshine!" This colloquialism possibly derives from board games like snakes and ladders, in which players, through bad luck or poor judgment, have to move their pieces back to the starting point.

> *The meaning of the expression, "back to square one" is similar to "back to the drawing board," which means to go back and rethink a complete project or scheme. Aircraft designers during the Second World War used this phrase when a concept or even a whole design for a new machine proved unworkable and had to be started all over again.*

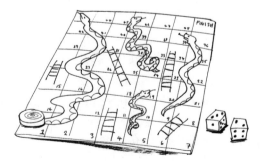

BAKER'S DOZEN

A baker's dozen is 13, one more than the standard dozen.

This phrase is widely held to date back to medieval England. Henry III (1216-1272) instituted a reign called the *Assize of Bread and Ale* that called for the severe punishment of any bakers caught shortchanging customers. English bakers developed the habit of including an extra loaf of bread when asked for a dozen to ensure that if one were stolen, dropped, or lost, they wouldn't be accused of shorting their customers.

BALLPARK FIGURE

An estimate, or a budget figure, which might better be described as a "guesstimate."

The phrase "in the same ballpark" was originally used when two figures, the projected and the real figure, were reasonably close. Over time, the term has evolved so that the estimated figure itself is now known as a "ballpark figure."

BARKING MAD

Used to suggest raving insanity, this phrase is frequently shortened to simply "barking." The expression emerged at the beginning of the twentieth century.

Its derivation stems from its link with rabid or mad dogs, whose wild howls and yaps audibly betrayed their diseased state.

BARK UP THE WRONG TREE

To be totally off the mark, to waste energy following the wrong course of action, or to have one's attention diverted off the subject in hand.

The phrase dates back to the 1800s and neatly puns a dog's bark with tree bark. The phrase's origins stem from the American sport of raccoon hunting. The hounds of the hunting pack are trained to mark the tree in which the raccoon they are

pursuing takes shelter, and then to howl at its base until their master arrives to shoot the animal. The hounds may bark up at the wrong tree, however, if the raccoon has managed to evade them.

The expression first became popular in the early nineteenth century, appearing in the works of James Hall, Davy Crockett—himself a great raccoon hunter—and Albert Pike.

BASKET CASE

A derogatory slang term used to describe a mentally-ill person who is unable to function properly. Recently the term has also come to be used in referring to poorly run and failing organizations.

The term originated in the U.S. military in World War I and was slang for soldiers who had lost both arms and both legs and because of this needed to be carried in a basket by others. Ironically, the term became widely known through a bulletin aiming to curtail its use. The U.S. Command on Public Information in March 1919, on behalf of Major General M. W. Ireland, the U.S. Surgeon General wrote:

"The Surgeon General of the Army…denies…that there is any foundation for the stories that have been circulated…of the existence of "basket cases" in our hospitals."

BEAT AROUND THE BUSH

To approach a matter indirectly or in a roundabout way.
The expression has evolved from early hunting methods for catching birds. One team of hunters would approach the birds hiding in the undergrowth from the sides, so as to drive them into the path of another team, who would catch them with nets as they took off.

This task of literally beating the bushes in which the birds take shelter is still an important part of pheasant shooting today.

A BEE IN ONE'S BONNET

To be obsessed with a particular idea or notion, as though mentally all abuzz.

The expression, in the form of the variant "to have bees in the head," implying scattiness, was in circulation in the sixteenth century, for a reference to bees and crazed thought was recorded by the English poet, Court musician and entertainer John Heywood in 1546 in one of his collections of English proverbs.

It is thought that bees first met bonnets in the poem "Mad Maid's Song" by Robert Herrick, written in 1648:

For pity, sir, find out that bee,
Which bore my love away.
I'll seek him in your bonnet brave,
I'll seek him in your eyes.

BETWEEN THE DEVIL AND
THE DEEP BLUE SEA

Caught between two evils or dangers, in a dilemma with nowhere to turn. The saying may be of nautical origin, the "devil" being a term for a seam in the hull of a ship that ran along the waterline.

A commonly used modern phrase with a similar meaning is "between a rock and a hard place."

"Between the devil and the deep blue sea" could also have been inspired by the ancient phrase "to steer or sail between Scylla and Charybdis."

In Homer's Odyssey, *Scylla was a six-headed monster who lived in a cavern overlooking a narrow channel off the coast of Sicily; she seized sailors from every passing ship with each of her six mouths.*

On the opposite rock, Charybdis, another monster, lived under a huge fig tree, from where she sucked in and regorged the sea, forming a treacherous whirlpool.

In the poem, Odysseus sailed between these two perils, losing his ship in the whirlpool and the crew to Scylla. Only he survived—by clinging to the fig tree.

BEWARE GREEKS BEARING GIFTS

Sometimes expressed as "I fear Greeks even when they offer gifts" (Virgil, *Aeneid*, 29–19 BC), this saying has its roots in the story of Helen of Troy (see **the face that launched a thousand ships,** page 66) and the Trojan War.

After a ten-year siege of the city of Troy by the Greeks, one of the remaining Greek besiegers (the Odysseus of the previous entry) devised an ingenious plan to invade the city. He hid all his men in a huge wooden horse, which was left outside the city gates, and then the Greeks abandoned their posts. The Trojans mistakenly took the horse to be a tribute from their beaten enemy and in celebration took the gift to the heart of their stronghold.

When night fell, the Greek soldiers poured out of the horse and—having the element of surprise—were victorious in the final battle.

THE BIG APPLE

The well-known nickname for New York City.

The name was first coined in the 1920s by John J. Fitz Gerald, a reporter for the *Morning Telegraph,* who used it to refer to the city's racetracks and who claimed to have heard it used by black stable hands in New Orleans in 1921.

Black jazz musicians in the 1930s took up the name to refer to the city, especially Harlem, as the jazz capital of the world.

The epithet was then revived in 1971 as part of a publicity campaign to attract tourists to New York.

The sentiment behind "The Big Apple" is likely to be the idea of an apple as a symbol of the best, as in **the apple of one's eye** (see page 16), meaning someone or something that is very precious.

> *In the eighteenth century, the writer and politician Horace Walpole referred to London as "The Strawberry," being impressed by its freshness and cleanliness compared with foreign cities; he named his estate at Twickenham, Middlesex, Strawberry Hill, and founded there the Strawberry Hill Press.*

THE BIG ENCHILADA

The leader, the top man or woman, the boss.

The phrase crops up in the infamous Watergate tapes, referring to the then U.S. Attorney-General, John Mitchell, who led President Nixon's re-election campaign in 1972. Mitchell was later indicted on charges that he had conspired to plan the burglary of the Democratic National Committee's headquarters in the Watergate complex in Washington, D.C., and had then obstructed justice and perjured himself during the subsequent cover-up. He was convicted in 1974.

"The big enchilada" is a modernized version of earlier phrases that became popular in the mid 1970s, such as "big gun" or "the big cheese," both of which are used to describe VIPs, especially in business; a group of them may sometimes be facetiously described as *les grands fromages*.

BIG-STICK DIPLOMACY

A political catchphrase that describes diplomatic negotiations backed up by the threat of military force.

The term was brought to public attention in 1901 when then U.S. Vice-President Theodore Roosevelt revealed in a speech his fondness for the West African proverb "Speak softly and carry a big stick, you will go far." (Later, as President, he employed this philosophy successfully in the Alaskan boundary dispute of 1902–04.)

THE BIRDS AND THE BEES

A euphemism for human procreation that was probably inspired by songwriter Cole Porter, thanks to his 1954 composition, "Let's Do It":

Birds do it, bees do it,
Even educated fleas do it,
Let's do it, let's fall in love.

The phrase was used, often by embarrassed parents or teachers, as a means of avoiding dangerous words like "sex" or "sexual intercourse"; nowadays, it tends to be used ironically.

BITE THE BULLET

To undertake the most challenging part of a feat of endurance, to face danger with courage and fortitude, to behave stoically or to knuckle down to some difficult or unpleasant task.

The expression originated in field surgery before the use of anesthetics. A surgeon about to operate on a wounded soldier would give him a bullet to bite on, both to distract him from the pain and to make him less likely to cry out.

BITE THE DUST

To fall down dead.

The Scottish author Tobias Smollett was the first to put this expression in print in 1750, in his translation of Alain-René Le Sage's *Adventures of Gil Blas of Santillane*; while in Samuel Butler's 1898 translation of Homer's *The Iliad,* Achilles has the line:

Grant that my sword may pierce the shirt of Hector about his heart, and that full many of his comrades may bite the dust as they fall dying round him.

Another version of the phrase—"lick the dust"—had the same meaning and appeared in the original (1611) edition of the King James Bible.

The phrase was in common use during the Second World War, especially in the RAF; today, it is more often used to describe the failure of an idea, plan or task than death or injury.

TO THE BITTER END

To the last extremity, to the final defeat, or to the death. An affliction can be borne until the bitter end, meaning to the last stroke of bad fortune.

'Bitter end" is a mid-nineteenth-century nautical term for the end of a rope or chain secured in a vessel's chain locker. When there is no windlass (winch), such cables are fastened to bitts—that is, pairs of bollards fixed to the deck—and when the rope is let out until no more remains, the end is at the bitts: the "bitter end."

However, the phrase appears in the Old Testament in the context that we use today, and some etymologists believe that this is the true source of the expression:

Her end is bitter as wormwood, sharp as a two-edged sword.

Proverbs 5:4

BLACKMAIL

The crime of forcing or coercing a victim into a particular action by threatening to reveal substantially true information about a person to a family member, associates, or the public that would either embarrass, socially damage, or incriminate the victim.

The term originated in 19th century Scotland and northern England where clan chieftains ran protection rackets against Scottish farmers.

BLOOD, SWEAT AND TEARS

An emphatic description of the effort required to complete a challenging task. It is a concise form of a phrase used by Winston Churchill in his first speech to the House of Commons upon taking over as Prime Minister, on May 13, 1940.

Yet Churchill may have been inspired by a number of sources; some three centuries earlier, John Donne wrote in "An Anatomy of the World" (1611), "Mollify it with thy tears, or sweat, or blood"; while Lord Byron observed in *The Age of Bronze* (1823):

Year after year they voted cent per cent,
Blood, sweat and tear wrung millions—why? For the rent!

At the time of Churchill's assumption of the highest political office, British morale was at a low ebb: German forces had overrun Denmark, Holland and Belgium, and were in the process of conquering Norway and France. The prospect of victory over Germany looked increasingly unlikely.

Churchill's actual words were, "I have nothing to offer but blood, toil, tears and sweat," and he revisited this phrase several times during the war years.

BLOW HOT AND COLD

To be inconsistent, to have fluctuating opinions, or simply to be unable to make up one's mind.

The expression has its origins in the Aesop's fable that describes the experience of a traveler who accepted the hospitality of a satyr (one of the gods of the forest, a creature who is part goat and part man).

The chilly traveler blew on his cold fingers to warm them—and then blew on his hot broth to cool it. The indignant satyr ejected him because he blew both hot and cold with the same breath.

BLUE BLOOD

A translation of the Spanish phrase, "sangre azul," which is used to indicate nobility or noble descent. The phrase is said to have derived from some of the aristocratic families of Castile who boasted that they were purebred, having no link with the Moors, who had longed controlled the country, or any other group. A mark of this pure breeding, they claimed, was that their veins showed more clearly blue through their fairer skin. By the 19th century, the phrase had come into wide use in English.

A BONE TO PICK

This is a desire to discuss a difference of opinion, settle a misunderstanding about something disagreeable, or express a complaint. The bone is probably the bone of contention, metaphorically tossed between two dogs fighting over it.

Usage goes back to the middle of the sixteenth century, but the expression may well have come from an earlier phrase, "to have a crow to pluck," which was used at least a hundred years earlier; the crow in this instance symbolizing discord.

In Howell's Proverbs (1659) the phrase "to have a goose to pluck with you" is used in the same sense.

BONE UP ON

To study intensively, to engage in serious research into a particular subject, or to revise a subject comprehensively.

Some sources suggest that the phrase is an allusion to whalebone in a corset, which sculpts the shape and stiffens the garment, as a metaphor for the gaining of "hard knowledge."

Others believe it came from the Victorian practice of using bone to polish leather, and that it indicated a polishing or refinement of knowledge.

However, in the nineteenth century a publishing firm owned by Henry Bohn produced English translations of Greek and Latin classics that were widely used by students cramming for their exams—and it is possible that the expression "to Bohn up" may have evolved into "bone up."

BORN ON THE WRONG SIDE OF THE TRACKS

To be born on the wrong side of the tracks is a disadvantage, as it was the part of town deemed to be both socially and environmentally inferior.

The expression originated from when railway lines ran through the centers of towns. Poor and industrial areas were often located to one side of the railroad tracks because the prevailing wind would blow smoke from the railway and smog in that direction, leaving the better-off neighborhoods unpolluted.

The phrase is now used to refer to anyone who comes from a poor or rough background.

THE BOTTOM LINE

The main point of an argument, the basic characteristic of something, the actual value of a financial deal, or the nub or truth of the matter.

The phrase itself is an accounting term, and refers to the figure at the end of a financial statement, indicating the net profit or loss of a company.

"The bottom line" gained wide currency as a phrase during the 1970s, possibly because of its frequent use by Secretary of State Henry Kissinger. He spoke of "the bottom line" as the eventual outcome of a negotiation—ignoring the distraction of any inessential detail.

BREAK A LEG!

The theater is notoriously superstitious, and among actors it is deemed bad luck to wish a colleague "good luck" before going on stage. Instead, this phrase—a traditional, if somewhat black, euphemism—is employed to wish someone luck in a performance, especially on opening night.

There are a number of possible sources for the expression and the earliest recorded use is in fact German; Luftwaffe pilots in the Second World War would send each other off to fight with the cheery saying "*Hals und Beinbruch*," meaning "break your neck and leg."

The phrase was also used in English around this time to mean "make a strenuous effort," so it may have simply been an instruction to put on the best show you possibly could.

A more fanciful explanation is that the saying came from the assassination of President Abraham Lincoln in his private box at Ford's Theatre, Washington, D.C., on April 14, 1865.

The murderer, John Wilkes Booth, a reputable Shakespearean actor, escaped after firing the shot by leaping down on to the stage, breaking his leg in the process.

THE BUCK STOPS HERE

A declaration meaning "this is where ultimate responsibility lies."

The most likely origin for the phrase is the poker table, where a buckhorn knife was placed before the player whose turn it was to deal. "Passing the buck" meant passing responsibility on to the next player.

The phrase was made famous by U.S. President Harry S. Truman, who had it handwritten on a sign on his desk at the White House to remind himself and those around him that he alone had the ultimate responsibility for every decision of his administration.

Some twenty-five years later, President Jimmy Carter had the legend reinstated with the same idea in mind.

BUSINESS AS USUAL

This self-explanatory expression was widely used in Britain in the Second World War, and especially during the London Blitz and the blitzes on other major cities, when shops and businesses continued to open in spite of bomb damage. In the capital, "Business as usual" and "London can take it" were commonly scrawled defiantly on the walls of damaged buildings.

Winston Churchill popularized the phrase in 1941 in a speech at the Guild Hall in London when he said, "The maxim of the British people is: 'Business as usual.'"

BY THE SKIN OF ONE'S TEETH

By the narrowest margin. There are several metaphors with the meaning "only just" and many allude to body parts (for example, "by a hair's breadth'), emphasizing the physical danger of a given situation from which one might have just escaped.

"By the skin of one's teeth" specifically is a (slightly misquoted) biblical phrase that means to have suffered "a close shave":

My bone cleaveth to my skin, and to my flesh, and I am escaped with the skin of my teeth.

Job 19:20

❧ C ❧

CALL OFF ALL BETS

A summons to cancel all wagers, deriving from the racetrack and the betting shop; for instance, a bookmaker may call off all bets if he suspects that a race or other contest has been rigged.

In a widening of its meaning, the phrase is used to mean rejecting a complicated or disadvantageous issue.

In slang of the 1940s, however, it meant "to die"—indeed, the most final way of calling off all bets.

CAN'T HOLD A CANDLE TO

To be unable to measure up to someone. The phrase dates back to the time before electricity when part of the duty of an apprentice was to hold a candle so that the more experienced workmen would able to see what they were doing. If an apprentice could not even perform this low level task adequately, his status was quite low.

Sir Edward Dering used a similar phrase "to hold the candle" in his The fower cardinal-vertues of a Carmelite fryar, 1641:

"Though I be not worthy to hold the candle to Aristotle."

CARRY A TORCH

To suffer unrequited love. Since the late 1920s, this phrase has been used to describe a long-standing emotional attachment that is either undeclared or not returned.

The torch represents the flame of undying love, and this symbolism may come from depictions of Venus, the goddess of love, holding a burning torch.

A "torch singer" is (usually) a female who sings sentimental love songs. It is thought that the expression "torch song," in this sense, may have been coined by Broadway nightclub singer Tommy Lyman in the 1930s.

CASE THE JOINT

A slang expression from the criminal fraternity meaning to inspect or reconnoiter a building before attempting to rob it or break into it for some other nefarious purpose.

"Joint" in this context means "a building": an early twentieth-century colloquialism for a sleazy dive where opium could be smoked or, during the Prohibition era (1920–33), where illicit spirits could be bought and drunk. The word "joint" has since come to be generally applied disparagingly to almost any disreputable establishment.

CAST THE FIRST STONE

To be first to criticize, to find fault, to start a quarrel, or to cast aspersions on someone's character. In biblical times, the barbaric custom of capital punishment was to pelt heretics, adulteresses and criminals with stones and rocks in a public place.

The phrase is from John 8:7, spoken by Jesus to the Scribes and Pharisees who brought before him a woman caught in adultery. They said that according to the law of Moses, she should be stoned to death, to which Jesus replied: "He that is without sin among you, let him first cast a stone at her."

CAST PEARLS BEFORE SWINE

To offer something precious or of quality to someone who is perceived to be too ignorant or uncultured to understand or appreciate it. To show, for example, a brilliant idea or a work of art to an unappreciative audience or to the kind of person known as a Philistine.

(Philistines were warlike immigrants to Philistia in ancient Palestine, who fought the Israelites for possession of the land, and came to be stigmatized as an uneducated, heathen enemy; the term has since by extension come to mean anyone unreceptive or hostile to culture, especially someone who is smugly and boorishly so.)

The phrase itself comes from the New Testament (Matthew 7:6): "Give not that which is holy unto the dogs, neither cast ye your pearls before swine, lest they trample them under their feet."

CAT GOT YOUR TONGUE?

A question directed at a silent partner in a conversation to ask why they're not speaking.

The earliest written example appeared in 1911, according to the *Oxford English Dictionary*, but it may have been around since the mid-nineteenth century.

As to the phrase's origins, numerous theories abound; none firmly proved. Some argue that it must stem from ancient Middle Eastern punishment techniques, when liars" tongues were ripped out and then fed to kings" cats; while others cite the much-feared whip the "cat-o'-nine-tails" as the source of the phrase, insinuating that this nasty weapon, used to flog sailors, forced them into silence—both through fear and pain.

THE CAT'S PAJAMAS

This colloquialism first surfaced in the 1920s to describe something or someone superlatively good or top-notch and has retained its meaning for almost a hundred years.

Alternative sources suggest that the phrase may come from an early nineteenth-century English tailor E. B. Katz, who apparently made the finest silk pajamas, though there is little evidence to prove this is true.

"The cat's whiskers" and "the bee's knees" are phrases with similar meaning. In the 1920s, people played with phrases that linked animals to humans, and so we find "the kipper's knickers," "the snake's hips," "the elephant's instep" and so on.

In the last twenty years, modern imagination has taken this idea further, and we now have more ribald phrases such as the popular British term, "the dog's bollocks" (which is sometimes abbreviated to just "the dog's").

CATCH-22

A Catch-22 situation is a lose-lose situation; whichever alternative you choose, you can't win.

It is the title of Joseph Heller's highly regarded satirical novel published in 1955. The story centers on Captain Yossarian of the 256th U.S. Army Air Force bombing squadron in the Second World War, whose main aim in life is to avoid being killed. The best way for a pilot to achieve this was to be grounded due to insanity…

> There was only one catch and that was Catch-22, which specified that concern for one's own safety in the face of dangers that were real and immediate was the process of a rational mind. Orr [another pilot] was crazy and could be grounded. All he had to do was to ask and as soon as he did, he would no longer be crazy and would have to fly more missions.

CATCH FORTY WINKS

A colloquial term for a short nap or a doze.

Just why shutting one eye forty times has come to mean a quick snooze is unclear, but it could have something to do with the fact that the number forty appears frequently in the scriptures and used to be thought of as a holy number.

Moses was on the Mount for forty days and forty nights; Elijah was fed by ravens for forty days; the rain of the Flood fell for forty days, and another forty days passed before Noah opened the window of the ark. Christ fasted for forty days, and he was seen forty days after his Resurrection.

> *Busy people and politicians who work late into the night maintain their faculties by taking "power naps" to recharge their batteries.*

A CHIP ON ONE'S SHOULDER

To display an inferiority complex, to perceive oneself as an underdog, to have a grievance, often unjustifiably.

The expression is believed to have originated in about 1840 and may allude to a game of dare, in which a man challenges another to dislodge a chip—as in piece of wood—he carries on his shoulder.

A chip is also a figurative term for consequences, and so the phrase may be a warning to an adversary not to aim too high.

There is an ancient proverb, "Hew not too high lest chips fall in thine eye." By the late sixteenth century, this health-and-safety warning had become something of a challenge, a dare to a fearless woodcutter to look high up without regard to any falling chips of wood.

CLAM UP

To refuse to talk, to stop talking, to become silent. People are generally said to "clam up" when they are trying to defend themselves.

The phrase takes its origins from the closed shell of a live clam. At high tide, clams open their shells a little to allow seawater to filter through, so that they can feed. When the tide goes out, they close their shells tightly to retain the water and protect themselves from predators.

CLEAN ROUND THE BEND

Completely crazy or eccentric. The phrase was described by
F. C. Bowen in the *Oxford English Dictionary* in 1929 as "an
old naval term for anybody who is mad."

*The word "clean" is used in many different ways to describe
something complete, pure, unmarked or unreserved—for
instance, "clean bowled," "to make a clean break" or "to
make a clean breast of it."*

CLEAR THE DECKS

To remove everything not required, especially when preparing
for action; to prepare for some task by removing the extrane-
ous or irrelevant.

This is a nautical phrase and alludes to a sailing ship preparing for battle, when anything in the way of the guns and their
crews, or that might burn or splinter, or that was not lashed
down, was removed from the usually cluttered decks so that
no untethered articles would roll about and injure the seamen
during the battle.

This saying is used in many contexts, such as clearing the
table of food and dishes or preparing the house to receive
guests.

"Deck" appears in many commonly used phrases, among them "to hit the deck"—to fall over, usually to escape injury—or "to deck someone" (to hit them and knock them to the floor).

CLIMB ON THE BANDWAGON

To declare support for a popular movement or trend, usually without believing in the movement or trend.

The expression is believed to have originated in the South, probably dating from the first presidential campaign of William Jennings Bryan in 1892, when candidates for political office would parade through the streets, led by a band of musicians performing on a large horse-drawn dray.

As a publicity stunt, the local candidate would mount the wagon as it passed and ride through his constituency in an attempt to gain personal support from the voters. Perhaps unsurprisingly, Bryan never won the presidency, losing to McKinley in 1896 and 1900, and to Taft in 1908.

The phrases "Get on the bandwagon!" and "Jump on the bandwagon!" are also often used.

CLOAK AND DAGGER

Any operation that involves some intrigue, especially the melodramatic undercover activities of those involved in espionage or other secret work.

Cloak-and-dagger plays were swashbuckling adventures popular in the seventeenth century. In France, a performance of this type was known as a *comédie de cape et d'épée* and this is the direct source of the English phrase, "cloak and dagger."

The name also appears in the Spanish comedias de capa y espada, *literally "comedies of cloak and sword," particularly those by the Spanish dramatists Lope de Vega and Calderón, although their plays were dramas of merely domestic intrigue.*

ON CLOUD NINE

To be on cloud nine means to be in a state of elation, very happy indeed, or feeling "as high as a kite."

This fanciful twentieth-century expression comes from the terminology used by the U.S. Weather Bureau. The Bureau divides clouds into classes, and each class into nine types.

Cloud nine is cumulonimbus, a cumulus cloud that develops to a vast height, with rounded masses of white vapor heaped one on the other; the upper parts resembling the shapes of domes, mountains or towers, while the base is practically horizontal.

CLUTCHING AT STRAWS

Someone in desperate circumstances will reach out and grab hold of anything, however flimsy or inadequate, in the hope of surviving the situation.

It was first used in print by Sir Thomas More in 1534, in his *Dialogue of Comfort Against Tribulation*.

The word "straw" has been used as a metaphor for years, representing the insubstantial or groundless, as in a "man of straw," someone financially insecure or with a poor credit rating. We also have "the last straw (that broke the camel's back)," that little extra burden which makes something no longer bearable (as with the camel's load, tipping the balance of tolerance).

COCK-AND-BULL STORY

A rambling or incredible tale; a tall story invented as an excuse; a lie.

There are various possible explanations for the derivation of this term. In the coaching days of the seventeenth century, the London coach changed horses at the Bull Inn and the Birmingham coach at the Cock Inn. The waiting passengers of both coaches would exchange stories and jokes. The "Cock-and-Bull" story is said to have originated from this scenario.

The phrase may derive, however, from ancient fables in which cocks and bulls and other animals conversed. In his Boyle Lecture of 1692, Richard Bentley stated:

> That cocks and bulls might discourse, and hinds and panthers hold conferences about religion.

While in his novel *Tristram Shandy* (1759), Laurence Sterne wrote:

> "L—d!" said my mother. "What is all this story about?"
> "A Cock and Bull," said Yorick—"And one of the best of its kind, I have ever heard."

Today both words are commonly employed separately in a slang or vulgar context. "Bull" is used as in "what a load of bull," politely avoiding saying the word "bullshit," while "cock" speaks for itself.

A Scottish satire or lampooning story is known as a "cocka-lane," which is taken directly from the French phrase of the same meaning as "cock and bull": coq et l'âne (cock and ass, donkey or fool).

COLD ENOUGH TO FREEZE THE BALLS OFF A BRASS MONKEY

This means that the weather is extremely cold, and although the expression sounds delightfully vulgar, it was not in fact originally a reference to monkeys' testicles.

A brass monkey is a type of rack in which cannonballs were stored. Being brass, the "monkey" contracted in cold weather, resulting in the cannonballs being ejected.

The expression has also mutated to a shortened form, again a comment on the temperature, as "brass-monkey weather."

COME OUT OF THE CLOSET

To declare one's homosexuality, to come out into the open about it. The term was used by the gay rights organization the Gay Liberation Front from about 1969, but the idea of "coming out" had first been encouraged by German gay-rights advocate Karl Heinrich Ulrichs in 1869.

In the days when homosexuality was a criminal offense, gay men had to hide the nature of their sexual preferences. They became known as closet queens, the closet being a private room.

When antihomosexual laws were repealed, the need for secrecy receded and gay men were able "to come out"—although many, fearful of society's disapproval, remained "in the closet."

The expression is now often used generally to mean "to declare one's real position."

> *The phrase "to come out" is also used to describe debutantes, upper-class young women making their official debut in society.*

COME UP TO SCRATCH

To be good enough to pass a test; to make the grade. This is a colloquialism from the boxing ring dating back to the nineteenth century.

Under the London Prize Ring Rules introduced in 1839, a round in a prizefight ended when one of the fighters was knocked down. After an interval of thirty seconds, the floored fighter was given eight seconds to make his way, unaided, to a mark scratched in the center of the ring.

If he failed to reach the mark, he had not "come up to scratch" and was declared the loser of the bout.

COUCH POTATO

Slang from the late 1980s, used to describe someone who indulges in the habit of lounging at home watching television, eating and drinking, but never exercising.

The expression is now used in most English-speaking countries, particularly with the increase in the number of television channels to choose from.

Perhaps the potato featured in the metaphor because the blemishes on its skin are known as "eyes"; or possibly because it is the tuber of the potato plant, punning with "the tube"—the television.

CROSS THE RUBICON

To take an irrevocable step, to burn one's bridges, to go beyond the point of no return.

The Rubicon was a small river, possibly the present-day Fiumicino, which formed the border between ancient Italy and Cisalpine Gaul, the province allocated to Julius Caesar. When Caesar crossed this stream in 49 BC, he went beyond the limits of his own province and became an invader in Italy, making the outbreak of war between Pompey and the Senate inevitable.

"The Rubicon" is now often used alone as a description of "the point of no return."

CRY ALL THE WAY TO THE BANK

The expression "to cry all the way to the bank" was a popular catchphrase in the 1950s. It is an ironic comment, usually made about someone who has done something questionable, or produced something kitsch or tasteless or for some reason generally disapproved of, while making a great deal of money from it.

It is thought to have been first used by the high-camp pianist and entertainer Liberace in 1956, after critics had savaged his performance at a Madison Square Gardens concert. Liberace was the highest-paid entertainer in the United States during the 1960s and 1970s, and his income averaged $5 million a year for more than twenty-five years.

CUT THE MUSTARD

A zesty and confident phrase meaning to do something well and efficiently, to prove oneself beyond all expectations at completing a task or occupation.

The expression probably derives from mustard as slang for "the best"; a line from O. Henry's *Cabbages and Kings* (1894) reads:

I'm not headlined in the bills, but I'm the mustard in the salad just the same.

"To cut," in this phrase, might refer to the harvesting of the plant, but it also might be used as in the expressions to "cut a dash," "cut up rough" or "cut capers."

CUT YOUR COAT ACCORDING TO YOUR CLOTH

This metaphorical proverb dates back to the sixteenth century and is all about good housekeeping and living within one's means. It is sensible advice to keep to one's budget and restrict expenditure to the amount of one's income.

It is often shortened, becoming simply "to cut your coat."

CUTE AS A BUTTON

To be charming, pretty, or attractive in a dainty way, almost always with the connotation of being small.

This often used simile sounds odd when you think about it. After all, how is it that a button is cute? That's debatable. Some say the "button" referred to here is not the kind you find on a shirt but actually the flower bud on a bachelor's button. Others insist the phrase refers to the button quail, an adorable little gray, fluffy bird.

D

DEAR JOHN LETTER

A "you're dumped" note from a wife or girlfriend breaking the news that the relationship with the recipient is over.

The expression originated during the Second World War. The unfortunate objects of Dear John letters were usually members of the armed forces overseas, whose female partners at home had made new liaisons, proving that absence sometimes does not make the heart grow fonder.

The name "John" was often used to signify "everyman" at the time; "John Doe" was the name given to any man whose real name was unknown or had to be kept anonymous.

THE DOG DAYS OF SUMMER

Very hot and oppressive summer days. The Romans called the hottest weeks of the summer *caniculares dies,* and not because dogs are thought to go mad in the heat (although Noël Coward did write in 1932 that "mad dogs and Englishmen go out in the midday sun").

The theory was that the days when the Dog Star, Sirius— the brightest star in the firmament—rose with the sun were the hottest and most sultry. It is an ancient belief that the combined heat of Sirius and the sun produced the stifling weather from about July 3rd to August 11th.

We also now use the phrase "dog days" to describe any period of stagnation.

DON'T COUNT YOUR CHICKENS BEFORE THEY'RE HATCHED

Don't assume something is certain before it is proved to be so. The phrase has been around for thousands of years, since it appears in Aesop's fable of "The Milkmaid and Her Pail."

There are probably more versions of this proverb than any other. "The man that once did sell the lion's skin / While the beast liv'd, was kill'd with hunting him," wrote Shakespeare in Henry V *(1598–9; 4:3), while a Hindu proverb urges, "Don't bargain for fish which are still in the water," and an ancient Egyptian saw cautions, "Do not rejoice over what has not yet happened."*

DON'T LOOK A GIFT HORSE
IN THE MOUTH

(see also **straight from the horse's mouth**, page 148)

This references the method of assessing the age of a horse by inspecting the length of its teeth. The meaning is: Do not question the value of something given to you. It is very bad form to inspect a gift for faults or defects, so be grateful for anything received. As the old saying goes: "It's the thought that counts."

The phrase is an old proverb that has been in use for hundreds of years. It was discovered in the writings of St. Jerome, one of the Latin Fathers of the fourth century, who identified it as a common proverb. The saying also occurs in French, German, Italian, Spanish and other European languages, emphasizing the centuries-long dominance of the horse until the coming of the automobile.

DRESSED TO THE NINES

To be dressed flamboyantly.

Some say that the phrase originated as tailors used to traditionally use nine yards of material to make a fine suit.

It is also worth noting that the shorter phrase, "to the nines," was used in the 18th century meaning achieving perfection or the highest standards. For example from William Hamilton's Epistle to Ramsay, 1719:

The bonny Lines therein thou sent me,
How to the nines they did content me.

DROP OF A HAT

On signal, instantly, without delay.

The expression alludes to the frontier practice of dropping a hat as a signal for a boxing or wrestling match to begin, usually the only formality observed. Athletics or horse races also used to be started by the fast downward sweep of a hat.

There are many sayings including the word "hat," such as "hats off to him," "as black as your hat," and "I'll eat my hat," all of which probably originated in the days when dress codes and social etiquette were more formal, requiring people in polite society to cover their heads.

~ E ~

EASY AS PIE

Making a pie is not easy and this expression must apply to the eating of it. It originates in the nineteenth-century, when sweet pie was a common dish and the word "pie" was associated with simple pleasures.

An easy task can also be described as a "piece of cake," which is also easy to obtain and eat, as opposed to baking it.

EAT HUMBLE PIE

To make a humble apology or to submit oneself to a certain degree of humiliation, to climb down from a position one has assumed, to be obliged to take a lower station.

Here, "humble" could be a play on the word "umble," the umbles being the offal—the heart, liver and entrails—of an animal, usually the deer, considered a delicacy by some, although most thought them only fit for the servants.

Though the word humble has a different derivation, the closeness of the two words could be one of the reasons the phrase evolved as it did. For when the lord of the manor and his family dined on venison at high table, the huntsman and lower orders of the household took lower seats and partook of the umbles made into a pie.

James Russell Lowell observed in 1864:

Disguise it as you will, flavor it as you will, call it what you will, umble pie is umble pie, and nothing else.

EGG ON ONE'S FACE

To be embarrassed or humiliated by something you have done.

The phrase has been used in the United States for over fifty years, and it seems to be a simple analogy that has become an idiom in itself. Just as if you were to eat your eggs sloppily and end up with them on your face, when you do something ineptly, you wind up looking foolish and embarrassing yourself.

AT THE ELEVENTH HOUR

Just in the nick of time, at the last moment, before the end of the day.

The allusion is to Jesus's parable of the laborers hired to work in the vineyard in which those starting work at the eleventh hour—that is, late in the afternoon at about five o'clock—were paid the same as those who had "borne the burden and heat of the day" (Matthew 20:1–16).

The Allies' armistice with Germany, ending the First World War, came into effect at the eleventh hour of the eleventh day of the eleventh month in 1918.

EVERY CLOUD HAS A SILVER LINING

In every situation, no matter how seemingly hopeless and gloomy, there is always some redeeming brightness to be found if one takes the trouble to look for it—"while there's life, there's hope."

This optimistic guidance to look on the bright side has been around since Roman times (although one Latin proverb reads, "After the sun, the clouds").

The phrase is thought to have its origins in Milton's *Comus* (1634): the lady lost in the wood resolves not to give up hope and says:

Was I deceived or did a sable cloud
Turn forth her silver lining on the night?

EVERY DOG HAS ITS DAY

This is a commonly used phrase that seems to have first appeared in English in the writings of R. Taverner in 1539 and subsequently in those of Shakespeare:

Let Hercules himself do what he may,
The cat will mew, and dog will have his day.

Hamlet (1600; 5:1)

It means that everyone will have a chance one day; everyone will have a moment of success or of being important eventually. This sentiment has been expressed for thousands of years.

> *The Latin proverb reads* Hodie mihi—cras tibi, *"Today to me, tomorrow to thee." And another ancient old wives" tale states that: "Fortune visits every man once, she favors me now, but she will favor you in your turn."*
>
> *As a further example, Peter Pindar wrote in his* Odes to Condolence *(1792):*
>
> *Thus every dog at last will have his day—*
> *He who this morning smiled, at night may sorrow,*
> *The grub today's a butterfly tomorrow.*

AN EYE FOR AN EYE

Punishment equal to the crime, retaliation in kind, or simply getting even. The justification for this form of retribution comes from the Old Testament:

> Eye for eye, tooth for tooth, hand for hand, foot for foot.
>
> Exodus 21:24

Jesus referred to these words in the New Testament and put his own spin on their message, creating another commonly used expression, "to turn the other cheek":

> Ye have heard that it hath been said, An eye for an eye, and a tooth for a tooth: But I say unto you, That ye resist not evil: but whosoever shall smite thee on thy right cheek, turn to him the other also.
>
> Matthew 5:38–9

❧ F ❦

THE FACE THAT LAUNCHED
A THOUSAND SHIPS

The face is that of the legendary beauty, Helen of Troy, and the ships were the Greek fleet, which sailed for Troy to avenge the King of Sparta.

In Greek legend, Helen was the daughter of Zeus and Leda, and wife of Menelaus, King of Sparta. She eloped with Paris, Prince of Troy, and the angry Menelaus sent a thousand ships to lay siege to the city of Troy. The fabled Helen is now an archetype of female beauty.

The phrase itself was first written by Christopher Marlowe:

Was this the face that launched a thousand ships,
And burned the topless towers of Ilium?

Doctor Faustus (first published 1604)

A FEATHER IN ONE'S CAP

A personal achievement or honor to be proud of. The feather is a proud and visible emblem of victory and the gesture of putting a feather in your hat is almost universal in one form or another.

There is an ancient custom, widespread in Asia, among Native Americans and throughout Europe, of adding a feather to one's headgear to mark each enemy killed. Even today, a sportsman who kills his first woodcock puts a feather from the bird in his hat.

At one time in Hungary, the only people who could wear feathers were those who had killed Turks.

When General Charles Gordon, known as "Chinese Gordon," quelled the Taiping Rebellion in 1864, he was honored by the Chinese government with the "yellow jacket and peacock's feather."

FIDDLE WHILE ROME BURNS

To delay or vacillate or do nothing during an emergency or crisis—an allusion to Nero's reputed behavior during the burning of Rome in AD 64.

Nero Claudius Caesar was the infamous Roman emperor whom his contemporaries believed to be the instigator of the fire that destroyed most of the city. As the blaze raged, it is said that he sang to his lyre and recited his own poetry, while enjoying the spectacle from the top of a high tower.

Many historians doubt his complicity, however, and Nero himself blamed the Christians.

FIFTEEN MINUTES OF FAME

Meaning to have short-lived fame, of the type that is now quite possible in the modern, media-driven, celebrity-obsessed age. The expression comes from the celebrated words of Andy Warhol, first published in a catalog for an exhibition of his work in Stockholm in 1968. Pop artist Warhol was concerned, among other subjects, with the nature of celebrity, and he wrote, "In the future, everyone will be world famous for fifteen minutes."

The phrase struck a chord and is often now shortened to "he's had his fifteen minutes."

IN FINE FETTLE

To be in good order or condition—"fettle" is an old word meaning condition, order or shape. Nowadays, it rarely appears on its own, being usually heard in the alliterative phrase.

In the past, we might have heard "good fettle" or "bad fettle," and in *John Barleycorn* by Jack London, published in 1913, he wrote:

> Those fifty-one days of fine sailing and intense sobriety had put me in splendid fettle.

The origin of the word "fettle" is somewhat obscure. It probably comes from the Old English fetel for a belt, so "fettle" first meant to gird oneself up, as for a heavy task.

The word was most typically used as a verb meaning to put things in order, tidy up, arrange, or prepare. Such as in Anne Brontë's *Agnes Grey* (1847), in the Yorkshire dialect speech of a servant:

> But next day, afore I'd gotten fettled up—for indeed, Miss, I'd no heart to sweeping an' fettling, an' washing pots; so I sat me down i' th' muck—who should come in but Maister Weston.

In northern English dialects, "fettle" is sometimes used in the sense of making or repairing something. In Australia, a "fettler" is a railway maintenance worker.

It is also used in some manufacturing trades—in metal casting and pottery it describes the process of knocking the rough edges off a piece.

FLAVOR OF THE MONTH

A generic advertising phrase of the mid 1940s attempting to persuade shoppers to buy a new flavor of ice cream each month and not just stick to their usual choice.

Since then, it has been used to describe any short-lived fashion, craze or person that is quickly dropped after a period of being in demand.

THE FULL MONTY

Everything, the lot, the complete works. Said of anything done to the utmost or fullest degree.

The origin of the expression is uncertain. It may derive from the "full amount"; or the Spanish card game *monte* (literally mountain or heap of cards); or it may refer to the full, three-piece, "Sunday best" suit from the men's outfitters Montague Burton.

The phrase became even more popular after the release of the hit 1997 film *The Full Monty*, directed by Peter Cattaneo. The movie followed a fictitious group of unemployed factory workers from Sheffield, England, who raise money by staging a strip act at a local club and taking off "the full monty."

AT FULL TILT

At full speed or with full force.

The expression probably originated in the fourteenth century, when "tilting at the quintain" was a popular sport among medieval knights. A dummy head, often representing a Turk or Saracen, was fastened to rotate around an upright stake fixed in the ground. At full speed, the knight on horseback tilted toward the head with his lance. If he failed to strike it in the right place, it would spin round and strike him in the back before he could get clear.

Tilting at the quintain remained a rustic sport, especially popular at wedding celebrations, until the mid-seventeenth century.

The similar phrase "to tilt at windmills" has a rather different meaning, namely "to battle fanciful enemies." The reference is to the crazed knight Don Quixote (in Miguel de Cervantes's novel, Don Quixote, *1605), who imagined the windmills to be giants and advanced to attack.*

❧ G ❧

GIVE SHORT SHRIFT

To treat someone peremptorily and unsympathetically, without heeding any mitigating arguments, or simply to make short work of something.

Shrift is defined as a confession to a priest. "Short shrift" originally referred to the limited amount of time given to a convict between condemnation, confession and absolution, and then finally execution.

GIVE THE THIRD DEGREE

To subject one to uncomfortably detailed questioning to get to the bottom of an inquiry, whether it be criminal or general.

One possible source of the phrase is Free Masonry, where the third degree is the highest level of membership. Those wishing to be considered as Master Masons must sit an intensive exam with interrogatory-style questions.

The term is applied to the use by the police of exhaustive questioning to extract a confession or incriminating information from a suspect, criminal, accomplice or witness.

"Third-degree treatment" is also used as a euphemism for torture.

GOOD OL' BOY NETWORK

This is the network of social connections established through the private-school system that were traditionally used to get on in life.

The old-school tie worn by former pupils of various private schools was a distinguishing mark, recognized by members of the same privileged class. That recognition would lead to favorable support and opportunities.

Today the old-boy network is seen in a negative light as a way of preserving the social elite.

GO OFF HALF-COCKED

To be unsuccessful at doing something due to inadequate preparation, or being in too much of a hurry—reminiscent of the phrase "more haste less speed."

The term is related to hunting and shooting and originates from the eighteenth century, when a musket that was cocked halfway had the hammer set in the safety position to prevent accidental discharge. However, the mechanisms were sometimes faulty and the gun would fire, much to the surprise of the musketeer.

Modern sporting guns cannot in fact "go off" at half-cock accidentally, as they no longer have a half-cock mechanism.

GOODY TWO SHOES

A goody two shoes is someone who is virtuous in a coy or sentimental way.

In 1765 a fable called the *History of Little Goody Two Shoes* was published. A variation on the Cinderella story, it is about a poor orphan girl who has only one shoe. She is so delighted when a rich gentleman gives her a pair of shoes that she keeps repeating that she has two shoes:

> She ran out to Mrs. Smith as soon as they were put on, and stroking down her ragged Apron thus, cried out, "Two Shoes, Mame, see two Shoes." And so she behaved to all the People she met, and by that Means obtained the Name of Goody Two-Shoes.

GRAND SLAM

A sweeping success or total victory.

This phrase surprisingly has its origins in a game of cards and not sports as one might guess. In the card game, contract bridge, the term refers to a high score involving winning all the tricks in a hand, and it contrasts with a "small slam." Now popularly used in a variety of sports, including golf and tennis, it used when a single player wins several major championship contests. In baseball, it refers to a home run with three runners on base.

THE GREEN-EYED MONSTER

To be jealous of or to covet someone's beauty, achievements, attainments or wealth. The metaphor is commonly reduced to the expression "to be green with envy." The monster was identified by Shakespeare in *Othello* (3:3):

> O! beware, my lord, of jealousy;
> It is the green ey'd monster which doth mock
> The meat it feeds on.

However, to accuse someone of having "green in their eye" is to suggest that they are inexperienced or easily bamboozled, as in "greenhorn," which means to be a novice, green behind the ears; like the green horns of a young horned animal.

Shakespeare again, in *Antony and Cleopatra* (1:5):

> My salad days,
> When I was green in judgment…

❧ H ❧

THE HAIR OF THE DOG

This phrase refers to a remedy usually administered to someone with a hangover, after an overindulgence of alcohol the night before. The theory is that the very thing that causes the malady is the best cure or means of relief, so another drink in the morning is considered by some the best pick-me-up (by others a recipe to make one feel worse, not better).

The general principle that "like cures like" comes from Roman times, expressed in Latin as *similia similibus curantura*. The peculiar "hair of the dog" phrase perhaps originated in the sixteenth century. Back then, if one was bitten by a mad dog (which was likely to be suffering from rabies), it was accepted medical practice to dress the wound with the burnt hair of the dog, as an antidote.

Amazingly, this cure was recommended for dog bites for about two hundred years before its efficacy was finally brought into question.

HAVE A FIELD DAY

A figurative expression for a day or occasion or time of particular excitement, often a day away from the usual routine.

The phrase is in fact a military term for a day when troops have maneuvers, exercises or reviews—out in the field. (The military refer to the area or sphere of operations as "the field.")

The term is now used more generally to mean a time of enjoyment, or making the most of things; we might say that the tabloid newspapers would "have a field day" if they got hold of a particularly salacious story.

In the U.S. Navy, "a field day" is a day devoted to cleaning the ship in preparation for inspection.

Students, meanwhile, enjoy field trips, on which they travel away from school, particularly to study geography.

HEEBIE JEEBIES

An expression of intense apprehension, anxiety, or depression.

To give someone the heebie jeebies is to make that person uncomfortably nervous.

The first known use of the phrase was in the 1920s during a period when nonsensical rhyming phrases, such as, "the bee's knees," seemed all the rage. Cartoonist Billy DeBeck is widely cited as coining this particular one in a 1923 cartoon of his in the October 26th edition of the *New York American*:

> You dumb ox—why don't you get that stupid look offa your pan—you gimme the heeby jeebys!

HERE'S MUD IN YOUR EYE!

A drinking toast, the sentiments of which could be read either way. One interpretation is that it is to wish good fortune, as it was used in the trenches of the First World War when soldiers would naturally rather mud was thrown in their eye than anything more lethal.

Another, somewhat less good-natured, theory comes from horse racing, in which, with one's own horse out in front, it will be kicking mud into the eyes of the slower runners behind.

The phrase itself is thought to originate from a Bible story—featured in chapter nine of the Gospel of St. John—when Jesus puts mud in the eyes of a blind man and restores his sight.

HOIST WITH ONE'S OWN PETARD

To be beaten with one's own weapons, or to be caught in one's own trap. The modern equivalent relates to the sport of soccer, "to score an own goal."

Shakespeare coined the phrase when he wrote these lines for Hamlet:

For 'tis the sport to have the engineer
Hoist with his own petard.

Hamlet (1600; 3:4)

In 1600, a petard was a newly invented explosive device used for blowing up walls, barricades or gates with gunpowder. It was a metal bell-shaped grenade filled with five or six pounds of gunpowder, dug into a trench and set off by a fuse.

The devices were often unreliable and went off unexpectedly, and the engineer who fired the petard might be blown up by the explosion. So the expression, in which "hoist" means to be lifted up, is an understated description of being blown up by your own bomb.

The name of the device came from the Latin petare, *meaning to break wind; the phrase is perhaps an ironic comment on the noise of the explosion.*

HUE AND CRY

A noisy commotion over some crowd gathering spectacle.

The phrase must have been in use since the beginning of the last millennium because the Norman French word *huer* means "to shout."

Until the beginning of the nineteenth century, "hue and cry" was the old legal term for an official outcry made when calling out for assistance, "with horn and with voice," in the pursuit of a suspected criminal escaping arrest. All able-bodied men were legally required to join the pursuit—if they refused, they risked being held liable for any theft committed by the fleeing felon. Thieves failing to respond to the "hue and cry" were liable to greater penalties once they were caught.

We now chiefly use the phrase to describe the way the news media clamor for someone to be held responsible for high-profile crimes or political mistakes.

HUNG, DRAWN AND QUARTERED

The correct order for this form of torturous capital punishment was that the victim was "drawn, hanged, drawn, beheaded and quartered." The crime that merited this sort of penalty was high treason.

The guilty were to be "drawn" to the place of execution on a hurdle or dragged along by horse's tail. Yet "drawn" also meant to be disembowelled, and this was added to the punishment in between the hanging stage and the beheading stage.

This expression is also sometimes shortened to just "drawn and quartered."

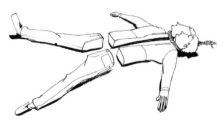

I

IT'S ALL GREEK TO ME

"It's all Greek to me" is used to mean that something is completely unintelligible to the speaker, Greek being a particularly tricky language to grasp because of its different alphabet.

The saying may have started out as an Anglicized version of the Latin phrase *Graecum est; non legitur,* meaning "It is Greek; it cannot be read," which was often used by monk scribes in the Middle Ages, when Greek was falling out of use.

It was probably popularized by Shakespeare's Julius Caesar, in which Casca says, "For mine own part, it was Greek to me" (1:2).

IT'S AN ILL WIND

Similar in spirit to "every cloud has a silver lining," this ancient nautical proverb suggests that some good can come from most misfortunes. The full phrase is, "It's an ill wind that blows nobody any good," meaning that only the very worst situations are universally bad, and that hardships usually bring benefits eventually.

It was already widely used by 1546, when John Heywood included it in his book of English proverbs. In 1591, Shakespeare wrote in *Henry VI*: "Ill blows the wind that profits nobody" (2:5).

IT TAKES TWO TO TANGO

A frequently used axiom that comes from the 1952 song of this title by Al Hoffman and Dick Manning:

> There are lots of things you can do alone!
> But it takes two to tango.

This satisfyingly alliterative phrase is often used in a sexual context when one partner is accused of seducing the other; it implies willingness on both sides. In general, it indicates that in any troublesome situation in which two people are involved, the blame should usually be shared between them.

It is also now used more widely in the fields of business and politics to imply that, in order to achieve agreement between two groups, both may have to compromise.

❧ J ❦

JUMP OUT OF THE FRYING PAN
INTO THE FIRE

To leap from one bad predicament to another which is as bad or even worse.

In English, the phrase can be traced back to about 1530 when, in the course of a religious argument, Sir Thomas More, Henry VIII's Lord Chancellor and author of *Utopia*, said that William Tyndale, translator of the Bible into English, had "featly conuayed himself out of the frying panne fayre into the fyre."

Unfortunately, both men met a gruesome end. Sir Thomas More was hanged as a traitor in 1535 for refusing to approve the marriage between Henry VIII and Anne Boleyn, while Tyndale was publicly strangled and burned as a heretic in 1536.

Most languages have an equivalent phrase for "to jump out of the frying pan into the fire"; the French have tomber de la poêle dans le feu—*"fall from the frying pan into the fire'— from which the English is probably translated. The ancient Greeks had, "out of the smoke into the flame"; the Italians and Portuguese, "to fall from the frying pan into the coals"; and the Gaelic is, "out of the cauldron into the fire."*

❧ K ❦

KEEP ONE'S POWDER DRY

To be prepared for action, but preserve one's resources until they are really needed. The phrase comes from a saying attributed to Oliver Cromwell, and the powder is, of course, gunpowder, which will not ignite if wet, or even damp.

During his savage Irish campaign of 1649, Cromwell is said to have concluded a speech to his troops, who were about to cross the River Slaney before attacking Wexford, with the rousing words, "Put your trust in God, my boys, and keep your powder dry."

There is no contemporary recording of his use of this phrase, however, and it is possible that it was coined later by the soldier and historian Valentine Blacker in his poem "Oliver's Advice," which attributed the line to Cromwell.

KEEPING UP WITH THE JONESES

This phrase defines twentieth-century materialism as the never-ending struggle to keep up with the apparent affluence of one's neighbors, paying particular attention to the cars they drive, the vacations they take, the schools their children attend and all sorts of other lifestyle indicators.

Arthur R. Momand ("Pop"), whose strip cartoon was first published in the *New York Globe* in 1913, probably invented the phrase, which he used as his cartoon's title. The strip was based on Momand's own experiences of living beyond his means in a prosperous neighborhood—and his realization that all his neighbors were doing the same as he.

KISS THE BLARNEY STONE

A popular term used of someone who speaks in persuasive or seductive terms; the verb "to blarney," meaning to employ persuasive flattery, and the noun "blarney," for "flattering talk," have the same derivation.

The provenance for this expression can be found, literally, at Blarney Castle, near Cork, in southwest Ireland. Set high in the south wall of the castle is an almost inaccessible triangular stone bearing the inscription, *Cormac McCarthy fortis me fieri fecit*.

The tradition of kissing this Blarney Stone to improve one's eloquence and persuasive abilities—which can only be done by hanging, with one's feet securely held, head-down from the castle's battlements—dates from the eighteenth century.

The story behind the Blarney Stone's legacy is that in 1602, McCarthy, Lord of Blarney, was defending the castle against the English, who were fighting to force him to surrender the fortress and transfer his allegiance to the English crown.

However, McCarthy smooth-talked the British emissary, Sir George Carew, with flattery and sweet promises and stood his ground, much to the fury of Queen Elizabeth I.

It is said that the Queen herself coined the term "blarney" to describe the worthlessness of McCarthy's promises.

KISS OF DEATH

This phrase derives from Judas Iscariot's kiss given to Christ in the Garden of Gethsemane before he betrayed him (Luke 23:48 and Matthew 26:49). It's also known as a "Judas kiss," meaning an insincere act of courtesy or false affection.

In Mafia circles, a kiss from the boss may indeed be a fatal omen.

The phrase is often used today in political or business contexts, meaning that certain associations or actions may prove to be the undoing of a person or organization, or the downfall of a plan or project.

KITCHEN-SINK DRAMA   87

KITCHEN-SINK DRAMA

A type of drama popular in the 1950s, in which the plot centers on the more sordid aspects of working-class or lower-middle-class domestic life. Much of the action takes place in the kitchen or at the kitchen sink, which presumably is a metaphor to suggest drudgery and the dullness of dirty dishwater.

Plays such as *Look Back in Anger* (1956; this play gave rise to the phrase, "angry young men") by John Osborne used such squalid settings to emphasize their message of protest against the established values of the time.

More recently, Joanna Trollope's stories of domestic dramas and upheavals feature the lives of the middle-class country set. Her books are known as "Aga sagas," because much of the action takes place near the comfort of this famous stove, seen in most country kitchens **worth their salt** *(see page 164).*

❧ L ❧

THE LAND OF NOD

In the Bible, this was the land to which Cain was exiled after he had slain Abel (Genesis 4:16), but in modern usage, the phrase refers to the unknown place we go to in our dreams.

Jonathan Swift, the famous satirist, was the first to use the phrase in its figurative context in his little-known work, *Complete Collection of Genteel and Ingenious Conversation* (1731–38)—usually referred to as *Polite Conversation*—in which he wrote that he was "going to the land of Nod," meaning that he was going to sleep.

"To nod off" also means "to fall asleep," though this term is largely derived from the fact that the head tends to nod forward when one feels drowsy.

LICK INTO SHAPE

To take a failing object or faltering venture and turn it into something that works effectively.

Centuries ago it was held that bear cubs were born shapeless and had to be properly formed by their mother's licking. The origin of this phrase dates back to a 1413 translation of Guilleville's *The pylgremage of the sowle:*

> Bears are born foul and misshapen and are subsequently formed into their natural shape by the licking of their father and mother.

LIE ON A BED OF NAILS

A situation or position, usually self-inflicted, that is fraught with a multitude of difficult problems.

The phrase refers to the spiked bed of the Hindu *sadhu* (ascetic or holy man), on which he chooses to sleep as a mark of spiritual devotion. But while the spikes may not hurt the *sadhu*, they would be unbearable for most normal mortals.

The saying is sometimes used in its variant form, "to lie on a bed of thorns"; both are used to describe painful situations that people have created for themselves.

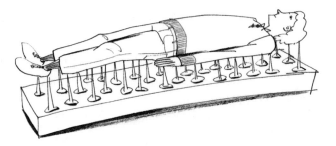

IN THE LIMELIGHT

To be in the limelight is to be the center of attention.

Limelight itself is an intense white light made by heating a piece of lime in a flame of burning oxygen and hydrogen. Thomas Drummond began using this process to create a bright light in the 1820s. It then became a widely used in theaters to illuminate the stage. Naturally the actors on stage were the center of attention, they were said to be in the limelight.

LIKE A BAT OUT OF HELL

Moving extremely quickly or suddenly.

Clearly referring to the rapid darting movement of bats, this phrase came into use at the turn of the twentieth century when Charles Earle Funk remarked that bats avoid light as if it were cast by the fires of hell.

LITTLE RABBITS HAVE BIG EARS

A twentieth-century Australian modification of the old proverb "little pitchers have great ears." The "ear" of a pitcher is the handle, which is often ear-shaped. The phrase "asses as well as pitchers have big ears" is also common.

They all mean that grown-ups should watch their language when talking in front of small children, who often pick up many a hint that the speaker might wish to have passed unnoticed.

LIVE LIFE IN THE FAST LANE

This is a metaphor meaning to live dangerously, indulgently and expensively, and dates from the late 1970s, probably coined by newspaper headline writers.

The fast lane is the inner lane of a highway, where traffic overtakes or travels at high speed. It is naturally associated with fast cars, and in an advertisement for Toshiba computers in 1989 the strapline read, "Jackie Stewart lives life in the fast lane—like any businessman really." (Stewart was three times the Formula 1 World Champion.)

The opposite metaphor, of course, is to be stranded on the hard shoulder of life.

❧ M ❧

MAD AS A HATTER

A renowned simile ever since Lewis Carroll's *Alice in Wonderland* (1865), although it can be found in W. M. Thackeray's *Pendennis* (1850) and is recorded as early as 1836.

The likely reason for linking hat-makers with madness is that hatters used the chemical mercurous nitrate in the making of felt hats, and its side effects can produce trembling symptoms such as those suffered in St. Vitus's Dance.

It is believed that Lewis Carroll based his character on Theophilus Carter, a furniture dealer who was known locally as the "mad hatter" because he wore a top hat and devised fanciful inventions such as an alarm-clock bed, which tipped the sleeper to the floor when it was time to wake up.

It has also been suggested that the original mad hatter was Robert Crab, a seventeenth-century English eccentric, who gave all his belongings to the poor and ate only dock leaves and grass.

MAD AS A MARCH HARE

Lewis Carroll also refers to the madness of the March hare in *Alice in Wonderland:*

> The March hare will be much the most interesting and perhaps, as this is May, it won't be raving mad—at least not so mad as it was in March.

The phrase comes from the observation that hares run wild in March, the beginning of their rutting season, exhibiting excitable behavior such as racing and "boxing."

The phrase first appeared in print in the late fourteenth century in Chaucer's *Canterbury Tales*, and has remained popular ever since.

MAKE A BEELINE FOR

To make a beeline for something is to go directly toward it.

In observing the behavior of bees, we see that when a forager bee finds a source of nectar, it returns to its hive and communicates its location to the other bees. Remarkably, after receiving this information, the other bees are then able to fly directly to the nectar.

MAKE DO

An official morale-boosting slogan that has a special resonance for people of a certain age. The phrase, originally "make do and mend," was designed to encourage thrift and the repairing of old garments and furniture, rather than buying a brand-new replacement and using up scarce resources.

It was in common use by 1943 and set the tone for life during the Second World War, and for many years after while food and clothing continued to be rationed.

The slogan struck a chord in the collective psyche, and although it may seem somewhat quaint to younger members of today's consumer society, the economic downturn has led to something of a revival in old-fashioned frugality.

MAKE HAY WHILE THE SUN SHINES

To act promptly when the opportunity presents itself and make use of favorable circumstances (see **strike while the iron's hot**, page 148). It has a similar seize-the-day meaning to the phrases "one today is worth two tomorrows," and, as seen on a postcard, "there's many a lemon dries up unsqueezed."

The phrase originated when many people worked on the land, and appeared in the sixteenth century. Before the days of the baler, cut hay was tossed about with a pitchfork before being gathered in, and then had to be left to dry in the fields, which meant that rain would spoil it.

In more recent times, it has come to be used as a justification for having fun or relaxing whenever the opportunity presents itself.

MAKE NO BONES

To be honest and direct without any risk that the statement may be misunderstood, but also sometimes used to mean to have no scruples about something.

One often cited source for this phrase is the world of gambling. Dice were often known as "bones" because they were originally made from animal bone. Yet there is no further evidence to link the phrase to dice.

It is more likely that it has its roots in the older expression "to find bones in something," which was used from the fifteenth century. That phrase came from the fact that finding bones in a bowl of broth was considered troublesome, so to find bones in something came to mean to take issue with it.

MEND FENCES

To rebuild a previously good relationship with someone you have had a disagreement with.

This expression is likely derived from the mid-seventeenth century proverb, "Good fences make good neighbors."

An early documented use of the phrase comes from a speech made by Senator John Sherman upon returning to his home in Mansfield, Ohio, in 1879. Sherman said, "I have come home to look after my fences."

❧ N ❧

NAUGHTY BUT NICE

Between 1981 and 1984 the British National Dairy Council used this alliterative and somewhat suggestive slogan in a campaign to promote fresh cream cakes and the phrase is now used for anything that is a little bit wicked but enormously pleasurable.

The novelist Salman Rushdie claimed on the BBC's *Desert Island Discs* that he had created the phrase when he was an advertising copywriter in London, but his claim was refuted by others who had worked on the account.

The phrase was certainly not new even then, since it was the title for a 1939 film about a classical-music professor who accidentally wrote a popular song, and the film starred Dick Powell and Ronald Reagan.

It has also been used as an oblique phrase implying sexual intercourse since about 1900.

NECESSITY IS THE MOTHER OF INVENTION

An imperative need will force one to summon extra creative forces to devise a solution, or to create something, to alleviate a problem.

The phrase is thought to have been used in some form by Plato in the fourth century BC in *The Republic,* but it first appeared with the modern wording in a 1671 comedy by William Wycherley.

More modern derivations of the phrase are "A guilty conscience is the mother of invention" and "Boredom is the mother of invention." And in a twist by one Thorstein Veblen, "Invention is the mother of necessity."

However, Daniel Defoe wrote in Serious *Reflections of Robinson Crusoe* (1720):

Necessity makes an honest man a knave.

THE NINETEENTH HOLE

The bar at the golf clubhouse. The standard golf course has eighteen holes, so the golfer who has played badly can drown his sorrows at the nineteenth. The term was first used by golfers in the 1920s.

NO HOLDS BARRED

Without rules or restrictions, often specifically referring to fighting, such as wrestling, hand-to-hand fighting, or martial arts.

The phrase originates with professional wrestling, and the holds referred to here are wrestling holds. Each type of wrestling has a specific set of rules attached to it. The sport has long been an Olympic one, administered by FILA, the sport's governing body. A match where no holds are barred is one where all of these rules and regulations have been lifted, and the fight is free form.

NO NEWS IS GOOD NEWS

The absence of information justifies continued optimism; that is, if all's quiet, then there is no cause for alarm. The phrase probably dates back to the early seventeenth century; in 1616, King James I wrote: "No newis is bettir than evill newis."

The word "news," now understood as a singular noun, was still plural up to the nineteenth century, as seen in this letter from Queen Victoria to the King of the Belgians, August 20, 1861: "The news from Austria are very sad, and make one very anxious."

The word is in fact short for "new stories," and the old spelling was "newes," a literal translation from the French *nouvelles*.

NOSE TO THE GRINDSTONE

To focus diligently on the task at hand.

This phrase is thought to have originated with knife grinders. They would sharpen blades by bending over stone, at times lying flat on their stomachs while keeping their faces near the grindstone.

NOT MY BAG

A slang expression for something that is definitely not one's subject or style.

It probably came from the jazz scene, "bag" meaning a personal style of playing; for instance, "playing with a hip-hop band was not his bag."

It shares a meaning with the more common phrase "not my cup of tea," which has been used throughout the twentieth century to denote something that isn't to one's taste.

NUDGE NUDGE, WINK WINK,
SAY NO MORE

A catchphrase understood by everyone during the 1970s, which came from the British TV comedy show *Monty Python's Flying Circus,* broadcast between 1969 and 1974.

Laden with sexual innuendo, these words provided the accompaniment to personal questions such as, "Is your wife a goer, then, eh, eh?" asked by a lewd character played by Eric Idle in a ridiculously suggestive manner, accompanied by much elbow jerking, embarrassed twitching and prodding.

O

AS OLD AS METHUSELAH

This means to be very old indeed. Methuselah is the oldest man referred to in the Bible, and it is written in Genesis (5:27) that he died at the impossibly great age of 969 years.

"As old as the hills" is another simile with a similar meaning as hills are indeed extremely ancient features of the landscape.

ONCE BITTEN, TWICE SHY

A phrase meaning that one learns from previous experience. Having been caught out once, one is wary or cautious the next time—and you should therefore learn from your mistakes.

"He that stumbles twice at the same stone deserves to have his shins broke" appears in R. Taverner's list of *Proverbs and Adages* of 1539, while the humorist Josh Billings said that "nobody but a fool gets bit twice by the same dog."

The idea behind the phrase is often attributed to one of Aesop's fables, which includes the line (as translated by William Caxton): "He that hath ben ones begyled by some other ought to kepe hym wel from the same."

ONE MAN'S MEAT IS ANOTHER MAN'S POISON

This is a very old adage that simply means that what is palatable or beneficial to one person is distasteful or harmful to another.

In ancient times, meat and bread were generic terms for food.

The phrase "different strokes for different folks" pretty well sums up the meaning. The rhythm and phrasing of this expression in particular have given rise to an endless stream of imitations. To an adulterer, perhaps, "One man's mate is another man's passion," or even "One man's Jill is another man's thrill."

The proverb's meaning in general has also inspired spinoffs. "One man's floor is another man's ceiling" is attributed to D. Bloodworth, while a contemporary version has a more political ring—"one man's terrorist is another man's freedom fighter."

OUT FOR THE COUNT

Said of someone who is fast asleep, dead drunk or completely demoralized.

It is a boxing and wrestling term describing defeat by being counted out by the referee. If a fighter is floored and does not find his feet within ten seconds counted out loud, he has lost the bout.

To say "count me out," on the other hand, means "do not include me in this."

OVER A BARREL

To be stuck in a helpless position, powerless to get yourself out of it, or to be at someone's mercy.

The phrase is possibly nautical in origin and is said to derive from the practice of draping over a barrel someone who has been rescued from the water when close to drowning, so encouraging the ejection of water from the lungs.

A more likely derivation, however, may be a form of punishment or torture in which the victim is bent over a barrel and beaten.

OVER THE TOP

An expression that describes something that goes way beyond the bounds of good taste or good sense, or which is outrageously inappropriate.

It came from the trenches of the First World War, when soldiers were described as going "over the top" when they scrambled out of the trenches to attack the enemy.

❧ P ❧

PAINT THE TOWN RED

To go out and party, to let your hair down and enjoy an uninhibited celebration, perhaps even to cause some disturbance in town.

This phrase, thought to have originated in the 1880s, may be an allusion to a town's red-light district; that is, the area where prostitutes ply their trade, advertising with red lights in the windows of their brothels, and where rogues might begin the evening before later extending the party to the rest of town.

Alternatively, it may have been a euphemism for a rowdy night in which blood would be spilled.

PANDORA'S BOX

This is a troublesome "can of worms"—a gift that seems of great value but is actually a curse, generating all sorts of unmanageable problems.

In Greek mythology, Pandora was the first woman, sent by Zeus as a gift to Epimetheus, who married her, against the advice of his brother Prometheus. As a wedding present, Zeus gave Pandora a beautiful box but instructed her that she must never open it. Over time, Pandora was tempted to defy this condition...but when she finally opened the box, all the evils of the world escaped, ever after to afflict mankind.

According to some, hope was the last thing that flew out; others believe that hope alone remained in the box.

> *The more modern phrase "to open a can of worms" is a graphic metaphor for a tangled, squirming, unpleasant or uncontrollable situation that had not been apparent beforehand.*

PASS THE ACID TEST

Said of someone or something that has been subjected to a conclusive or severe test.

The phrase was used literally during the gold rush, when prospectors needed a sure-fire way of telling gold from valueless metals. Gold is not attacked by most acids, but reacts to nitric acid, also known as *aqua fortis*, which is therefore the acid used in the "acid test" for gold.

To "put on the acid" is probably derived from "to pass the acid test" and is Australian slang meaning to exert pressure on someone when asking for a favor or a loan.

PASS THE BUCK
(see also **the buck stops here**, page 36)

To evade blame or responsibility and shift all criticism else-where. A phrase from the game of poker, the "buck" being the token object that is passed to the person whose turn it is to deal the next hand.

Originally, the token was a buckhorn knife, so called because its handle was made from the horn of a buck, or male deer (although some sources argue that the buck was either a piece of buckshot or a buck's tail, which early hunters carried as a talisman).

The earliest recorded use of the phrase is by Mark Twain in 1872, in the first decade after the end of the Civil War (1861–65), when poker or "stud poker"—the stake was probably originally a stud horse—were played in bars by lumberjacks, miners and hunters, those being the days before it became known as a "gentleman's" game.

PASS MUSTER

To come up to an adequate standard, to pass inspection or to get by. Originally, "muster" was a military term for the gathering of soldiers for roll call and inspection.

To "muster in" means to enroll, and to "muster out" means that the group disperses or falls out.

PAST THE SELL-BY DATE

This term comes from the supermarket and is applied to perishable foods. The dates before which, for safety reasons, the goods should be sold and consumed are indicated on the packaging.

The expression is widely applied metaphorically to almost any short-lived or disposable area of life that may lose its freshness or appeal, such as ideas, fashion, relationships; it is sometimes also used of people, especially those in high-profile jobs, such as actors or models.

PEANUT GALLERY

An audience that gives a performer a difficult time with interruption and jeering.

This term has its origin in the days when vaudeville theater was popular. The cheapest seats in such theaters at the time came to be known as the peanut gallery, and this where the crowd was often loudest and most rowdy.

FOR PETE'S SAKE

An exclamation of annoyance or impatience. Just who Pete is exactly remains a mystery.

The expression is perhaps an oath in the name of St. Peter, the guardian of the Gates of Heaven. Saying "for Pete's sake" might be an entreaty to the person you're saying it to; that is, they should consider the fact that St. Peter might judge them for their actions. Alternatively, it may have evolved from "for pity's sake."

Nowadays, this particular expression of exasperation is not so frequently heard because the threshold of acceptability for more blasphemous expletives is far lower.

A PIG IN A POKE

To buy a pig in a poke is to purchase something before you have seen it and verified its worth.

The phrase derives from an ancient form of trickery when animals were traded at market and a small suckling pig was taken for sale in a "poke"—a word shortened from the word "pocket," which was a stout sack.

Sales had to be agreed without opening the poke, supposedly for fear of the lively piglet escaping. Rather, people used the sealed sacks to try to palm off the runts of the litter to unsuspecting buyers, and sometimes even cats were substituted for pigs.

If the less gullible purchaser insisted on seeing the contents of the poke, the salesman might literally have to "let the cat out of the bag" (therefore, that other well-known expression), and the game was up.

This form of suspicious market trading has been around for hundreds of years and is referred to in Thomas Tusser's *Five Hundred Good Pointes of Husbandrie* (1580).

> *The practice was obviously widespread because other languages have similar expressions—such as the French* chat en poche—*which also refer to the folly of buying something without seeing it first. The Latin proverb* caveat emptor— *"let the buyer beware"—warns against such underhand techniques.*

A PINCH OF SALT

To take something with "a pinch of salt" is to treat information or explanations with great reservation, qualification, scepticism, doubt or disbelief.

A version of this phrase, "take with a grain of salt," was in use from the seventeenth century, and is thought to stem from the popular notion that taking a small amount of salt with other ingredients was a good antidote for poison.

PLEASED AS PUNCH

In the traditional comic puppet show *Punch and Judy*, the pompous Mr. Punch gloats smugly at the success of his evil actions and superiority over his shrewish wife, Judy, and it is from this scenario that the phrase originates. Punch had a lot to be pleased about; his quick wit was triumphant even over the Devil.

The present Punch and Judy *scenario is similar to the original by the Italian comedian Silvio Fiorello, dating from about 1600. Although the basic plot varies, it usually involves Punch's enraged bludgeoning of his wife, Judy, their child, and several lesser characters, followed by his imprisonment…and escape, thus him being "pleased as Punch."*

The violence of the storylines is counteracted by slapstick action and comic dialogue.

POUR OIL ON TROUBLED WATERS

A well-known metaphor meaning to mollify or soothe with gentle words, or to use tact and diplomacy to restore calm after an angry or bitter argument.

It has been a well-known scientific fact since the first century AD that rough waves are calmed when oil is poured upon them. According to the Venerable Bede's *History of the English Church and People* (AD 731), St. Aidan, an Irish monk of Iona, knew of this "miracle" and gave a young priest a vessel of holy oil to pour on the sea when the waves became stormy. (The priest was on an important voyage to fetch a maiden destined to be the bride of King Oswy.)

Moreover, on his many Atlantic crossings between Pennsylvania and Portsmouth in the eighteenth century, the ever-curious Benjamin Franklin observed not only the Gulf Stream, but also the calming effect of oil on the waves.

PRETTY PLEASE

An emphatic way of asking for something often used by young children trying to be extra cute.

How can the word please be pretty you ask? Actually the word pretty has historically been used to mean more than just attractive, as in the phrase "pretty penny."

PRIDE GOES BEFORE A FALL

An ancient warning for the arrogant to avoid conceit; do not be too cocksure or big-headed because events may conspire to bring you down. The phrase is shortened from the passage in Proverbs (16:18):

Pride goeth before destruction, and an haughty spirit before a fall.

"Pride goes before, and shame comes after" is another form of the proverb as it was used in the sixteenth and seventeenth centuries. It has also been said that "he who gets too big for his britches gets exposed in the end."

PROOF IS IN THE PUDDING

To test the limits of something by trying it yourself.

This phrase actually derives from a longer phrase, "the proof of the pudding is in the eating." Now the phrase is often used in respect to flying aircrafts and taking them to the limits of their designated altitude and speed limits.

PUSHING THE ENVELOPE

To go beyond the standard and commonly accepted boundaries; to innovate.

This phrase actually does not refer to stationery, but to mathematics. In mathematics, the term envelope is defined as "the locus of the ultimate intersections of consecutive curves." As such it came to be used the upper and lower limits of flight patterns. To push the envelope was to test these limits while in flight.

PUT A SOCK IN IT!

A plea to be quiet, to shut up, to make less noise.

It comes from the end of the nineteenth and beginning of the twentieth centuries, when the early gramophones, or "phonographs," had large horns through which the sound was

amplified. These mechanical contraptions had no volume controls, and so a convenient method of reducing the volume was to stuff a woolen sock inside the horn.

PUT LIPSTICK ON A PIG

A term used to describe a weak attempt to deceive people by trying to make an ugly person or thing appear attractive.

This term, often used by politicians, derives from proverbs about attempting to make an ugly thing pretty. Similar phrases from the eighteenth century include, "a hog in armor is still but a hog."

PUT ON THE BACK BURNER

To put off or postpone. A very useful expression in business if a decision cannot be made immediately, meaning that an idea, proposition, course of action or project can be put aside and kept in reserve for use when necessary, or when circumstances are more propitious.

It stems of course from the back burners, or rings, of a stove, which are used for simmering, while the front burners are usually the hottest and used for fast cooking.

There is now even a verb form gaining increasing usage in office jargonese, with people talking of "back-burnering" something.

An almost diametrically opposed metaphor is also used: an idea or project can be "put on ice," to be figuratively defrosted at a later date.

PUT ONE'S FOOT IN IT

To make an inadvertent blunder, particularly to say the wrong thing and to embarrass oneself. To make a *faux pas*, which literally means "a false step."

The full phrase, from which this shortened version comes, is "to put your foot in your mouth," and several sources suggest that this was first used in reference to eighteenth-century Irish parliamentarian Sir Boyle Roche.

He famously delivered lines such as: "All along the untrodden paths of the future, I can see the footprints of an unseen hand." A contemporary is believed to have said of him, "Every time he opens his mouth, he puts his foot in it," and the phrase took off.

Prince Philip, who has something of a reputation for saying the wrong thing at the wrong time, calls the affliction "dentopedalogy."

ᔞ R ᔞ

READ THE RIOT ACT

Figuratively, "to read the riot act" is to attempt to quell chattering and general commotion or misbehavior, particularly in a group of children, by vigorous and forceful pleas coupled with threats of the consequences if order is not resumed.

The original Riot Act became British law in 1715, and stated that when twelve or more people were gathered with the intention of rioting, it was the duty of the magistrates to command them to disperse, and that anyone who continued to riot for one hour afterward was guilty of a serious criminal offense. It was not superseded until 1986 when the Public Order Act was introduced.

"To run riot" was originally said of hounds that had lost the scent and was later applied to any group that behaved in a disorderly or unrestrained way.

THE REAL McCOY

This is a common expression that originated in Scotland as "the real Mackay," meaning "the real thing."

Mackay was the name of an old family descended from the Scottish people known as the Picts; the term appeared in the *Scottish National Dictionary* in 1856 as part of the phrase "a drappie (drop) of the real Mackay."

In the 1880s, the expression was adopted as an advertising slogan for Mackay whisky, which was exported to the United States and Canada, where people of Scottish origin drank it and kept the phrase alive.

In the 1890s, it was applied to a famous boxer, the prize fighter Kid "the Real" McCoy, and this is the spelling that has remained in use.

Coca-Cola, probably the most advertised product in the world, adapted the phrase in the 1970s by describing their product as "the real thing" in comparison with any rival products.

REVENGE IS A DISH BEST SERVED COLD

Be patient, vengeance will be all the more satisfying if you take your time in getting back at someone.

There is an old proverb from 1578 that advises, "Living well is the best revenge," and according to Euripides (480–406 BC), "There's nothing like the sight of an old enemy down on his luck."

The modern wording of this phrase is often thought to come from the eighteenth-century French novel Les Liaisons Dangereuses by Pierre Ambroise François Choderlos de Laclos, as *la vengeance est un plat qui se mange froid.*

In fact, the phrase does not appear in the original novel and appears only in later adaptations.

> *The theme of revenge has featured in art since the early Greek dramas; the most famous example in English is perhaps Shakespeare's* Hamlet *(1600).*
>
> *This particular phrase was revived in 2003 as a tagline for Quentin Tarantino's revenge film* Kill Bill.

RING THE CHANGES

This phrase comes from the world of bell ringing, which became popular in the seventeenth century and remains so to this day. It means to make variations in the way you do something.

A "change," you see, is the order in which a series of bells is rung. Thus with a series of four bells, as in many parish churches, it is possible to ring twenty-four changes without once repeating the order in which the bells are struck ($4 \times 3 \times 2 \times 1 = 24$).

In the nineteenth century, the phrase took on a new meaning and was used to imply that someone had been paid back for a wrongdoing or practical joke, usually by being given a taste of his own medicine.

We now most commonly use the phrase to mean simply "to make changes" or "to try several changes."

The greatest number of changes ever actually rung on bells is reported to have been 40,320 changes on eight bells (8 × 7 × 6 × 5 × 4 × 3 × 2 × 1 = 40,320), which took about eighteen hours.

ROME WASN'T BUILT IN A DAY

Great achievements, worthwhile tasks and the like are not accomplished without patient perseverance and a considerable passage of time.

This was originally a Latin proverb and has been quoted ever since, as in *A dialogue conteinyng the nomber in effect of all the prouerbes in the englishe tongue* (1546) by John Heywood:

Rome was not bylt on a daie (quoth he) and yet stood Tyll it was fynysht.

Rome was the greatest city in the ancient world and, according to legend, was founded in 753 BC by Romulus (therefore, the city's name) and his twin brother, Remus. However, it is most likely to have been named from the Greek *rhoma* meaning "strength"; its other Latin name is Valentia, from *valens* meaning "strong."

As an indication of its importance in the world, Rome features in numerous old sayings such as "When in Rome, do as the Romans do" and "All roads lead to Rome" (or "All roads lead to rum," as W. C. Fields put it).

ROUND ROBIN

A petition or protest signed in a circular form on the page so that no one name heads the list. The device is believed to have originated in seventeenth-century France, and the term could be a corruption of rond and ruban—round ribbon.

The round-robin letter is believed to have been adopted by British sailors in the seventeenth or early eighteenth centuries, for use when presenting a grievance to the ship's captain. To avoid punishment, the ringleader would arrange for the signatures to be inscribed in a circular fashion around the page— although if the ship's captain was particularly vindictive, he would punish all the signatories for insurrection.

Today we use the phrase to mean the opposite of its original meaning—it is rather a letter or email from a single author that is sent to numerous recipients.

A round-robin tournament is a friendly sporting contest, such as tennis, in which all participants change partners so that everyone competes against everyone else.

ROUND UP THE USUAL SUSPECTS

Since the film *The Usual Suspects* was released in 1994, this phrase has returned to regular use and is employed as a jocular instruction to gather a group of people together.

It is thought that the line was first spoken in the film *Casablanca* (1943), directed by Hal B. Wallis and starring Humphrey Bogart and Ingrid Bergman. Claude Rains, playing the French Captain Renault, chief of police in wartime Casablanca, delivers this classic line in a scene near the end of the movie: "Major Strasser has been shot. Round up the usual suspects."

When shooting began on Casablanca, *the script was not finished. Toward the end of filming, the dialogue was written on demand and literally rushed to the set.*

According to the film chronicler Leslie Halliwell, the film "just fell together impeccably into one of the outstanding entertainment experiences in cinema history."

THE ROYAL "WE"

The somewhat superior choice of the collective pronoun "we" in place of the individual "I" by a single person.

Legend has it that King Henry II was the first to employ the royal "we" in 1169 when justifying a decision to his barons; he argued that since kings were ordained by God, his choices were God's choices too, and so used "we" rather than "I" when issuing his orders.

The current Queen of England, Elizabeth II, often uses this style in referring to herself, for instance during her Christmas Day broadcasts, while the frosty comment "We are not amused" was attributed to Queen Victoria in 1900.

In March 1989, the then Prime Minister, Margaret Thatcher, announced to the world in a famously regal tone:

We have become a grandmother.

RUB SALT INTO THE WOUND

To increase someone's pain or shame.

The phrase alludes to an ancient nautical punishment for misbehavior by members of a ship's crew. Errant sailors were flogged on the bare back, and afterward salt was rubbed into the wounds. Salt is a well-known antiseptic, so it helped to heal the lacerations, but it also made them much more painful.

An extension of this phrase is the saying "Don't rub it in," an admission that one may have made a fool of oneself, but people should not carry on reminding one.

RULE OF THUMB

A rough guesswork measure, a calculation based on generally held experience in a certain field. This rule is distinct from any proven theory.

It refers to the use of the thumb to make rough measurements. The first joint of the average adult thumb measures 1 inch or 25 mm, so could be used to measure objects quickly that were close at hand; while raising the thumb and aligning it with distant objects was a common way of estimating how far off they were.

RUN THE GAUNTLET

To be attacked on all sides or, in modern use, to be severely criticized or to try to extricate oneself from a situation while under attack on all sides.

The expression appeared in English at the time of the Thirty Years War as "gantlope," meaning the passage between two files of soldiers. It is an amalgamation of the Swedish words *galop* (passageway), *gata* (way), and *lop* (course).

"Running the gauntlet" was a form of punishment said to have originated in Sweden among soldiers and sailors. The company or crew, armed with whips, thongs or rods, were assembled in two facing rows, and the miscreant had to run the course between them, while each man dealt him as severe a blow as he thought befitted the misdemeanor.

Native Americans also had a similar, more brutal, form of retribution, because here the victim was not intended to survive the blows he suffered during his run.

❧ S ❧

SAIL CLOSE TO THE WIND

This is another of the many proverbs that come from life on the high seas. It is a figurative term, still in use today, meaning to take a chance, to emerge from an escapade just within the letter of the rule book, or, more riskily, to push the limits of what decency or propriety allows.

The nautical expression refers to the practice of steering a ship as near as possible to the point from which the wind is blowing, while keeping the sails filled.

> To "sail against the wind" is to go against the trend, in opposition to current thinking, practice or fashion. And to "sail before the wind" is to prosper, to meet with great success, just as a ship sails smoothly and rapidly with a following wind.
>
> Similarly, to "sail into the wind" is to tackle a difficult task with great vigor and directness.

THE SANDS ARE RUNNING OUT

A metaphor to remind us that time is short; there will be less time to do what you have to do unless you act now. The phrase is frequently used with reference to someone who has not much longer to live.

The allusion is to the sand in an hourglass. The original version of the phrase is "the sands of time are running out," the first part of which appears in the poem "A Psalm of Life" (1838) by Henry Wadsworth Longfellow:

> Lives of great men all around us,
> We can make our lives sublime,
> And, departing, leave behind us
> Footprints on the sands of time.

Or as Robert Burns wrote in "Tam o" Shanter" in 1791:

> Nae man can tether time or tide.

This is a variant of the old (c. thirteenth-century) English proverb "Time and tide wait for no man."

SAVE ONE'S BACON

To have a narrow escape, to be rescued from some dire situation without injury or loss.

This expression dates from the late seventeenth or early eighteenth century when bacon was a significant part of the diet.

According to Nathan Bailey's *Universal Etymological English Dictionary* of 1720, "bacon" was also a slang term to describe booty of any kind that fell to beggars, petty thieves, highwaymen and the like in their enterprises. As such bacon became synonymous with livelihood, so "to save someone's bacon" therefore took the meaning "to save a person."

"To bring home the bacon," meaning to earn the money to maintain the household, describes the custom at country fairs of greasing a live pig and letting it loose among a group of blindfolded contestants. Whoever successfully caught the greased pig could keep it and so "bring home the bacon."

SAVED BY THE BELL

This is a boxing term thought to date from the late nineteenth century. A floored contestant being counted out (see **out for the count,** page 103) might be saved by the ringing of the bell marking the end of the round, giving him the three-minute break between rounds to recover.

However, there is another, albeit unsubstantiated, and rather gruesome theory to explain this phrase. When graveyards became overcrowded in the eighteenth century, coffins were dug up, the bones taken away and the graves reused.

In reopening the coffins, one out of twenty-five was found to have scratch marks on the inside, meaning that its occupant must have been buried alive.

To guard against this most unfortunate occurrence in the future, a string was tied to the wrist of the corpse, which led from the coffin and up through the ground, where it was tied to a bell. Someone would have to sit in the graveyard all night to listen for the bell—hence the phrase "saved by the bell."

From the same derivation, we have night workers on the "graveyard shift" and sailors on the "graveyard watch" between midnight and dawn.

SEE A MAN ABOUT A DOG

This is a very shifty turn of phrase and suggests a desire to cover up one's real actions. It is the excuse offered if one wishes to be discreet and avoid giving the true reason for leaving the room, the meeting or whatever social gathering.

The phrase is sometimes used as a euphemism for some unmentionable activity such as going to the lavatory—or worse, going to do something or meet someone one shouldn't.

The phrase originally referred to betting on dog racing.

SEE RED

To give way to excessive passion or anger, or to be violently moved; to indulge in physical violence while in a state of frenzy.

The reference is to the Spanish spectacle of bullfighting and the art of taunting the bull. The phrase "like a red rag to a bull" is said of anything that is calculated to excite rage. Toreadors" capes are lined with red (although there is actually no evidence to suggest that the color itself incenses the bulls).

The phrase may also have blended with term in use in the early 1900s, "to see things red," which describes the feeling of anger when the blood rises, or the "red mist" descends.

SEE THROUGH ROSE-TINTED GLASSES

To look at life or to regard circumstances with unjustified optimism, always looking on the bright side of life, as though it were suffused with a gentle pink light. Eyeglasses of such a hue would show the world "in the pink"—but it would be misleadingly rosy, bright and hopeful.

The French equivalent is *voir la vie en rose*—again, to see life "in the pink," which in turn means to be in excellent health (abbreviated from the phrase "in the pink of health" or "in the pink of condition," a definition derived from a flower in its best state).

SELL SOMEONE DOWN THE RIVER

This expression means to deceive or to betray. The phrase probably originated in the first few years of the nineteenth century in the South.

Since by then it was illegal to import slaves, there was an internal trade and they were brought down the Mississippi to the slave markets of Natchez or New Orleans. Therefore if a slave was "sold down the river," he lost his home and family.

The saying particularly alludes to the practice of selling unruly slaves to owners of plantations on the lower river, where conditions were harsher than in the more northerly slave states.

To "sell" is old slang for "swindle" or "hoax," and a person who has been tricked is said to have been "sold."

SELL OFF THE FAMILY SILVER

To dispose of long-held and valuable assets for immediate short-term gain. This phrase comes from a speech made by former British Conservative Prime Minister Sir Harold Macmillan to the Tory Reform Group in 1985.

Though in favor of privatization in principle, he objected to methods used by Margaret Thatcher's government and to the use of the profits of the sales of Britain's big industries as if they were income.

"First of all the Georgian silver goes, and then all that nice furniture that used to be in the saloon. Then the Canalettos go," he said, likening the process to the selling off of prized heirlooms by aristocratic families desperate for a quick injection of cash.

The term is now common shorthand for the selling of state-owned resources to private companies.

SEND IN THE CLOWNS

A last ditch effort to salvage a performance by trying to make the crowd laugh.

Having nothing to do with circus clowns, the phrase came into use when a song titled as such by Stephen Sondheim became popular in 1973. The song was written for the musical *A Little Night Music.* A character from the play sings the song as she reflects back on her life and thinks of how her choices in love were foolish. It is a song of regret.

SEPARATE THE SHEEP
FROM THE GOATS

To divide the worthy from the unworthy, the favored from the disfavored, the good from the bad. The phrase comes from the Bible, where sheep represent the flock of Christ, while goats symbolize virility, lust, cunning and destructiveness, and, often, the Devil.

> And before him shall be gathered all nations; and he shall separate them one from another, as a shepherd divideth his sheep from the goats.
>
> Matthew 25:32

A similar expression, also from the Bible, is "to separate the wheat from the chaff," meaning to distinguish good from bad. A more modern version is "to separate the men from the boys."

IN SEVENTH HEAVEN

To be supremely happy, in a state of complete ecstasy.

The seventh heaven was defined by the Kabbalists—students of a Jewish mystical system of theology and metaphysics with its roots in ancient Greek teachings, which dates from the eleventh and twelfth centuries, and from which Madonna's famous version of Kabbalah stems.

The Kabbalists interpreted passages from the Old Testament based on the symbolism of numbers, devised and decoded charms and created mystical anagrams and the like. They maintained that there were seven heavens each rising above the other; the seventh being the home of God and the archangels, the highest in the hierarchy of the angels.

Seven is a mystic or sacred number. It is the sum of four and three which, among the Pythagoreans, were, and have been ever since, counted as lucky numbers. Among ancient cultures, there were seven sacred planets.

The Hebrew verb "to swear" means literally to "come under the influence of seven things," while in an Arabic curse, seven stones are smeared with blood. All of which demonstrate the power of seven as a mystical number.

SHAKE A LEG

The summons "shake a leg" is a morning wake-up call. It is a naval phrase and was the traditional alarm call used to rouse the hands from their hammocks.

It comes from the days in the mid-nineteenth century when women were allowed to sleep onboard ship when the navy was in port. At the cry of "Shake a leg," if a woman's limb was shaken out of the hammock, she was allowed to lie in, but if the hairy leg of a rating appeared, he had to get up and get on with his duties.

Later in the nineteenth century, to "shake a leg" came to mean "to hurry up."

AT THE SHARP END

Directly involved with the action, positioned where the competition or danger is greatest. The connection is not with the point of a sword, but with the pointed shape of the bows of a ship, which are the first toward the enemy at the start of any engagement or battle.

The cry of "Look sharp!" or "Sharp's the word!" are both calls to immediate action, whether on the battlefield or in the playground; the expressions also mean to be observant, to "keep your eye on the ball."

Before the days of large supermarkets and closed-circuit TVs, if a shopkeeper suspected a customer of shoplifting, he would give a coded warning to his assistant by saying, "Mr. Sharp has come in."

SHOOT THE MOON

This is an expression meaning to leave without paying one's bills or rent, or to remove swiftly one's household goods under cover of night to avoid their seizure by a landlord or creditor. It's more colloquially known as "to do a moonlight flit" and is often shortened to "do a moonlight" or even "to flit." Another similar expression is "doing a midnight run."

Simply "to moonlight," however, means to take a second—secret—job, supposedly at night, to supplement one's wages from the day job.

References to the moon are often used to denote that something is fanciful: for instance, unrealistic ideas are known as "moonshine"; "to reach for the moon" means to crave what is totally beyond one's reach.

TO SIT ABOVE THE SALT

To sit in a place of distinction at the dinner table.

Formerly, the family "saler" or salt cellar was an ornate silver centrepiece, placed in the middle of the table. Special or honored guests of distinction sat above the saler—that is, between the salt and the head of the table where the host sat—while dependants and not-quite-so-important personages sat below.

THE SIXTY-FOUR-THOUSAND-DOLLAR QUESTION

The ultimate and most difficult question, the nub of a problem.

This widely used phrase comes from the 1940s radio quiz show, *Take It or Leave It*. During the course of the show, contestants were asked increasingly difficult questions for prize money, which also increased as the questions became harder. The final question was worth $64.

Naturally, inflation has affected this expression over the years since it began life as the humble sixty-four-dollar question, growing first to sixty-four thousand dollars and recently to sixty-four billion.

A SKELETON IN THE CLOSET

A domestic source of humiliation or shame that a family or individual conspires to conceal from others. Every family is said to have one, and certainly these days it seems that every public figure does too, whether it is in the form of an ex-mistress or lover, or some ancient but discreditable financial scam.

The expression seems to have been in use from the early 1800s and may have derived from the gothic horror stories popular at the time, in which murders were concealed by hiding the corpse in a cupboard, or bricking it up in a wall. In 1853, it appeared in the figurative sense in *The Newcomes* by William Makepeace Thackeray:

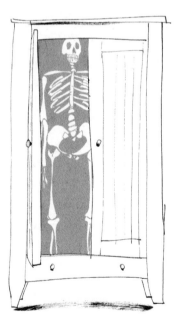

And it is from these that we shall arrive at some particulars regarding the Newcome family, which will show us that they have a skeleton or two in their closets as well as their neighbors.

An apocryphal source of the phrase is a story in which a person without a single care or trouble in the world had to be found. After a long search, a squeaky-clean lady was found, but to the great surprise of all, after she had proved herself on all counts, she went upstairs and opened a closet, which contained a human skeleton.

"I try and keep my trouble to myself, but every night my husband makes me kiss that skeleton," she said. She then explained that the skeleton was that of her husband's rival, killed in a duel over her.

ON SKID ROW

An expression applied to the part of town frequented by vagrants, hobos, alcoholics and down-and-outs. Hence if you are "on the skids," it means that you are on your way to that rather grimy quarter of the city, about to skid off the path of virtue and respectability.

The expression probably comes from the early days of the Seattle timber industry. A "skid row" was a row of logs down which other felled timber was slid or skidded. Tacoma, near

Seattle, became prosperous with the growth of the timber industry, and in due course there were plentiful supplies of liquor and brothels in the town, close at hand for lumberjacks working the skid row.

SLEEP TIGHT

Another way of saying good night and sleep well.

This phrase dates back to when beds were made of rope and straw. It is a shortened form of the expression, "sleep tight and don't let the bed bugs bite." Before going to sleep at night, people would have to pull the ropes tight in order to have a firm bed to sleep on as the ropes would have loosened during the course of the previous night's sleep.

SNUG AS A BUG IN A RUG

A whimsical and comfortable comparison dating from the eighteenth century, although a "snug" is a sixteenth-century word for a parlor in an inn.

The phrase is usually credited to Benjamin Franklin, who wrote it in 1772 as an epitaph for a pet squirrel that had belonged to Georgiana Shipley, the daughter of his friend, the Bishop of St. Asaph.

Franklin's wife had sent the Shipleys the gray squirrel as a gift from Philadelphia, and they named him Skugg, a common nickname for squirrels at the time. Tragically, he escaped from his cage and was killed by a dog. Franklin wrote:

Here Skugg
Lies snug
As a bug
In a rug.

However, there are earlier uses, as in a celebration of David Garrick's 1769 Shakespeare festival. Seen printed in the *Stratford Jubilee*:

If she [a rich widow] has the mopus's [money],
I'll have her, as snug as a bug in a rug.

And there are several similar variations from which the phrase may have sprung. In 1706, Edward Ward wrote in *The Wooden World Dissected*:

He sits as snug as a bee in a box.

And in Thomas Heywood's 1603 play *A Woman Killed with Kindness*, there is:

Let us sleep as snug as pigs in pease-straw.

SOUR GRAPES

This is an ancient metaphor used when someone denigrates something that is clearly desirable because they know they can't have it for themselves.

The phrase comes from the well-known fable "The Fox and the Grapes" by Aesop, dated to the sixth century BC:

> One hot day, a thirsty fox spotted some juicy-looking grapes hanging from a vine. The cluster of fruit was just out of reach. However hard he tried, he could not reach the grapes; and the greater the effort he made, the hotter and thirstier he became.
>
> Eventually, the fox gave up and reasoned that as the grapes were beyond reach, they would probably be sour and inedible.

The moral of the story is that we can console ourselves with the fact that, although some things are unattainable, we probably wouldn't like them anyway.

SPEAK OF THE DEVIL

Have you ever mentioned someone's name conversationally and then a few moments later that same person has unexpectedly walked into the room? At this moment you might exclaim, speak of the devil!

This is actually a shortened form of the phrase, "Speak of the devil and he doth appear." This original expression was an English proverb dating back to the Middle Ages. During this period there was a superstition that if you spoke of the Devil, or even of just mentioned evil in general, it may provoke the Devil to appear, bearing with him unfortunate consequences.

SPILL THE BEANS

The expression means "to let on," to tell all—perhaps prematurely—to an eager audience, to give away a secret or "to let the cat out of the bag" (see **a pig in a poke**, page 109).

There are various explanations for the derivation, one of the most colorful being that it may have originated at the turn of the twentieth century as a euphemism for vomiting, because beans represented basic food.

Another possibility is that the phrase comes from ancient Greek voting practices, where black and white beans were used to represent agreement and disagreement with the issue being voted on. Each voter put one bean into a pot or helmet—and the result was revealed by spilling out the beans.

> *Beans appear in various expressions: "To be full of beans" means to be in high spirits or full of energy, and was originally said of lively horses; beans used to be slang for money or property, so that "I haven't got a bean" means that one is broke.*

SPIN DOCTOR

This phrase comes from baseball and refers to the spin put on the ball by a pitcher to disguise its true direction or confuse the batter.

It is an idiom that was first applied in political commentary in the mid 1980s during Ronald Reagan's presidency, describing his public-relations advisers during promotion of the "Star Wars" Strategic Defence Initiative (SDI).

These so-called "spin doctors" were on "spin control," their mission being to give the preferred interpretation of events to the world's media, manipulating public opinion in the desired direction.

STAND IN ANOTHER MAN'S SHOES

"To stand in another man's shoes" is to take the place of another person empathetically.

In a similar vein, the opportunistic phrase "waiting for dead men's shoes" is sometimes thought, if not spoken.

Among the Vikings, when a man adopted a son, the adoptee put on the shoes of his new father.

Reynard the Fox, *a medieval beast epic (c. 1175–1250), is a satire on contemporary life found in French, Flemish and German literature. Reynard, having turned the tables on the former minister Sir Bruin the Bear, asks the Queen to let him have the shoes of the disgraced bear. As a result, Bruin's shoes are torn off and put on the new hero.*

STEAL SOMEONE ELSE'S THUNDER

To adopt someone else's own special methods or ideas as if they were one's own.

The story behind the origin of this phrase was recounted by the eighteenth-century actor-manager, playwright and Poet Laureate Colley Cibber in his *Lives of the Poets* (1753), and was also mentioned by Alexander Pope in his poem *The Dunciad* (1728).

Legend has it that John Dennis, an actor-manager of the early part of the eighteenth century, had invented a machine to make stage thunder, which he employed in his own play, *Appius and Virginia,* performed at the Drury Lane Theatre in London in 1709.

However, Mr. Dennis, whatever his inventive talents, was not a particularly gifted playwright; the play did not fill the house and was soon taken off in favor of a production of *Macbeth* by another company.

Dennis went to their opening night and was astonished to hear his thunder machine in action. He leaped to his feet and shouted, "That is my thunder, by God; the villains will play my thunder but not my play!"

Since the eighteenth century, the phrase has subsequently been refined to become "to steal one's thunder."

STIFF UPPER LIP

A determined resolve combined with complete suppression of the emotions.

This is supposedly a traditional characteristic of the English, especially military officers during the two world wars. Their upper lips were frequently concealed with a mustache, which perhaps became fashionable because it could conceal any uncontrollable trembling reflexes at the wrong moment. A quivering upper lip is often deemed a sign of emotion.

The phrase appeared well before the First World War in the work of poet Phoebe Cary in "Keep a Stiff Upper Lip":

And though hard be the task,
"Keep a stiff upper lip."

STILL WATERS RUN DEEP

However quiet or calm someone may seem on the surface, do not be deceived: there is probably great depth of knowledge, personality or a hot temper lurking below.

This is a Latin proverb, thought to come from Cato's Morals. The version we use today was first printed in an anonymously authored Middle English verse work "Cursor Mundi" ("Runner of the World"; c.1300), which includes the line: "There the flode is deppist the water standis stillist."

The Malayan proverb, "Don't think there are no crocodiles because the water is calm," means much the same.

It is never a good idea to show off or talk too much, because as everyone knows, empty vessels make the most noise. Speech is silver, but silence is golden.

STRAIGHT FROM THE HORSE'S MOUTH
(see also **don't look a gift horse in the mouth**, page 58)

Some knowledge received direct from the highest authority, from the person whose word need not be doubted.

The expression comes from horse racing, where the tips to be trusted came from those closest to the breeders and trainers. The phrase implies that you've heard something from the best possible source—in this case, the horse itself.

A variation on this as a source is the idea that the true age of a horse can be ascertained by an examination of its mouth. The first permanent horse teeth appear in the center of the jaw at the age of two and a half. A year later, a second pair appears, and at between four and five years, the third pair appears.

So, no matter what an owner may say about a horse's age, the evidence is in the horse's mouth.

STRIKE WHILE THE IRON'S HOT

To act immediately when the opportunity arises. This is a metaphor from the blacksmith's shop, since iron cannot be easily worked once it has cooled down.

The phrase has been attributed to Geoffrey Chaucer, although there are many ancient sayings that encourage action today rather than waiting for tomorrow. Pittacus said, "Know thy opportunity," while **make hay while the sun**

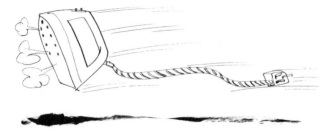

shines (see page 94) appears in an early sixteenth-century book of proverbs.

More up to date, a women's-lib slogan neatly inverts the proverb in a warning against inaction: "Don't iron while the strike is hot."

THE SWORD OF DAMOCLES

Impending danger or disaster in the midst of great prosperity or good fortune.

In the fourth century BC, Damocles, who was a toadying sycophant of Dionysus the Elder of Syracuse (see **the walls have ears**, page 159), was invited by the tyrant to test his self-proclaimed charm and wit. Damocles accepted and was treated to a sumptuous banquet, but over his head a sword was suspended by a mere hair, intended by Dionysus as a symbolic indicator of the fragility of wealth and power, his own included.

This quite naturally inhibited Damocles's performance at the banquet because he was too frightened to move.

T

TO A T

A way of describing that something is just right.

The origin of this phrase is debated. An early-recorded use comes from James Wright's satire *The Humours and Conversations of the Town* (1693):

All the under Villages and Towns-men come to him for Redress; which he does to a T.

This early reference may referred to a t-square used to make precise measurements.

TAKE A RAIN CHECK

A rain check is the receipt of a baseball ticket that can be used at a later date if a game has been interrupted by rain.

The phrase is now often used figuratively, to put an invitation on hold and defer it until a later date. It is, in fact, a polite way of postponing something indefinitely, with only a minor commitment to rearrange.

TAKEN FOR A RIDE

This colloquial phrase can be interpreted in one of two ways. It refers either to the victim of a light-hearted joke, prank or con, or—in its sinister and probably original meaning, a completely genuine use of the phrase—to someone who is taken for a ride somewhere and does not come back in one piece, if at all.

The rival underworld gangs of major cities in the 1920s and 1930s were virtually at war with each other, and any unfortunate who was unlucky enough to tempt the wrath of the gang leader, or Don in the case of the Mafia, would be literally taken for a ride in a limousine, ostensibly to discuss certain matters or sort out some misunderstanding. He would be very unlikely to return alive, however—or, indeed, to return at all.

TALK TURKEY

To discuss some subject frankly or seriously.

The origin of the expression is uncertain, but it is thought to date back to the nineteenth century and may have arisen from the efforts of turkey hunters to attract their prey by making gobbling noises. The birds would then either emerge from their cover or return the call, so revealing their whereabouts.

At the turn of the last century, the turkey was considered an amusing bird, and conversations in which one "talked turkey" were convivial. A young suitor's chat-up lines would also be called "talking turkey," perhaps because in a fit of nerves he might become tongue-tied and his words would come out like gobbling noises.

Later, the meaning became more serious and related to stern admonitions.

Incidentally, turkeys do not come from Turkey, but from North America, and were brought to Spain from Mexico. Benjamin Franklin suggested the turkey should be the national emblem; however, the bald eagle was chosen instead.

THICK AS THIEVES

To be intimate with some person or group, to be in collusion with them. "Thick" is used in this context to mean "closely knit."

Thieves notoriously conspire and plot together and devise secret languages so that they can discuss their business in a code that will not be understood by others—a slang or jargon that used to be known as "thieves Latin." Cockney rhyming slang itself was originally a closed language to the uninitiated and was created by crafty East Londoners to outwit authority and eavesdroppers.

"As thick as thieves" was already a common saying by the time it was first used in print in the 1800s, and we now use it primarily to describe people who are close friends.

THREE SHEETS TO THE WIND

To be very drunk.

This phrase was originally a seafaring expression. The sheets refer to ropes or chains fixed to the lower corners of sails in order to hold them in place. If three sheets are loose and blowing in the wind, the sails will flap, causing the boat to stagger about like a drunken sailor.

THROW IN THE TOWEL

To throw in, or throw up, the towel means to give up, to admit defeat. The metaphor is from prize-fighting, which predated modern boxing, and refers to a second from the boxer's corner tossing a towel, used to refresh his contestant in between rounds, toward the center of the ring, to signify that his man is beaten.

"To throw in the towel" also means to concede defeat in boxing, for a second might also literally throw a towel into the ring to show that the game is up.

THROW ONE'S HAT INTO THE RING

To enter a contest or to become a candidate for office.

This expression relates to the early nineteenth-century custom of throwing one's hat into the boxing ring to indicate that you wanted to take on the pugilist.

By the early twentieth century, the term was regularly used in professional boxing and in 1912 it became firmly linked to political ambition when Theodore Roosevelt announced his intention to run for the presidency by telling a reporter: "My hat's in the ring, the fight is on, and I'm stripped to the buff."

TOO MANY COOKS SPOIL THE BROTH

A well-known proverb meaning that too many opinions on a matter become self-defeating. The adage has been in use since the sixteenth century, if not before.

For almost every proverb or nugget of wisdom, however, there is usually another that means precisely the opposite: The usual riposte for "too many cooks spoil the broth" is "many hands make light work."

Groucho Marx once commented: *"I'm going to stop asking my cooks to prepare broth for me. Over the years, I've found that too many broths spoil the cook."*

TURN THE TABLES

To reverse a situation and put one's opponent in the predicament that one has been suffering. The saying was recorded in the early seventeenth century and was applied to the game of backgammon, the table or board on which it was played being known as "the tables."

The phrase may come from the old rumored custom of reversing the table, or board, in games of chess or draughts, so that the opponents' relative positions are altogether changed— but even then it had a figurative meaning, too.

In a sermon published in 1632, an English deacon called Robert Sanderson, who later became the Bishop of Lincoln, said:

Whosover thou art that dost another wrong, do but turn the tables: imagine thy neighbor were now playing thy game, and thou his.

~ U ~

UNDER THE TABLE

This phrase originated during the Second World War, and describes a—then very common—practice among businessmen.

From the outbreak of the war, many items, ranging from the basics like eggs, butter, meat and jam to "luxuries" such as gas, silk stockings and chocolate, were rationed. Dishonest businessmen would keep articles and foodstuffs that were in short supply out of sight or "under the table," for sale to favored customers, usually at inflated prices.

This form of trading was part of the thriving wartime black market, and the term is still used today to describe any illicit trading.

⚜ W ⚜

WALK THE PLANK

To be put to the supreme test or, worse, to be about to die.

"Walking the plank" is a nautical term for a punishment involving being made to walk blindfold and with bound hands along a plank suspended over the ship's side—one eventually lands up in the drink as shark food, if not drowned first. It was a pirate custom of disposing of prisoners at sea in the seventeenth century.

The practice is probably more familiar in fiction than in fact, however, since pirates would have been unlikely to kill off captives, who could have been sold as slaves or ransomed.

In R. L. Stevenson's novel The Master of Ballantrae *(1889), James Durie and Colonel Francis Burke enlist with the pirates who capture their ship, but the brigands make their other prisoners walk the plank.*

The infamous Captain Hook, in J. M. Barrie's Peter Pan and Wendy *(1912), meanwhile, threatened to flog Wendy and the Lost Boys with a cat-o'-nine-tails…and then make them walk the plank.*

THE WALLS HAVE EARS

This is a warning to watch what you say, or what secrets you divulge, wherever you are, because someone might be listening.

In the time of Catherine de'Medici, wife of Henry II of France, certain rooms in the Louvre Palace, Paris, were said to be constructed to conceal a network of listening tubes called *auriculaires,* so that what was said in one room could be clearly heard in another. This was how the suspicious queen discovered state secrets and plots.

The legend of Dionysus's ear may also have been the inspiration for the phrase. Dionysus was a tyrant of Syracuse (see **the sword of Damocles**, page 149) in 431–367 BC, and his so-called "ear" was a large ear-shaped underground cave cut into rock. It was connected to another chamber in such a way that he could overhear the conversations of his prisoners.

WASH ONE'S HANDS OF SOMETHING

To abandon something, to have nothing to do with some matter or person, or to refuse to take responsibility.

The allusion is to Pontius Pilate's washing of his hands after the trial of Jesus. Pilate was the Roman Governor of Judaea who tried Jesus. Although he found Christ not guilty, he washed his hands of the matter by bowing to the pressure of Jewish religious leaders and letting them decide Christ's fate:

> When Pilate saw that he could prevail nothing, but that rather a tumult was made, he took water, and washed his hands before the multitude, saying, I am innocent of the blood of this just person: see ye to it.
>
> Matthew 27:24

WHAT THE DICKENS?

An exclamation of surprise or disbelief, akin to "What the devil?" The phrase is often shortened to "What the...?"

"Dickens" here is probably a euphemism—one possibly in use since the sixteenth century—for the Devil, otherwise known as Satan or the Prince of Evil, and has nothing to do with the novelist Charles Dickens.

In Low German, its equivalent is "De duks," which may have become altered in English to "dickens."

The phrase was already in use by the time Shakespeare was writing:

I cannot tell what the dickens his name is.
The Merry Wives of Windsor (1600; 3:2)

> *"To play the dickens"* is an old-fashioned expression meaning to be naughty, or act like a devil.

WHAT IS GOOD FOR THE GOOSE IS GOOD FOR THE GANDER

This old phrase seems to promote sexual equality long before it was fashionable. It suggests that the same rules apply in both cases—what is fitting for the husband should also be fitting for the wife—though it is more likely that the phrase was used more generally to mean what is good enough for one person is good enough for another.

WHERE'S THE BEEF?

Advertising slogan meets political catchphrase. The Wendy hamburger chain's 1984 television commercial showed a group of elderly women looking at the small hamburger of a competitor on a huge bun—they all admired the bun, but the unimpressed third woman asked, "Where's the beef?"

Later in 1984, when Walter Mondale was seeking the Democratic presidential nomination, he famously quoted the slogan to describe what he thought was a lack of substance in the policies of his rival, Gary Hart.

The phrase is also used to mean "where's the problem?"

WHITE ELEPHANT

A useless and costly possession that cannot be disposed of because of some sort of value associated with it.

This term comes from Southeast Asia where white elephants are considered sacred. A gift of a white elephant is a sign of peace and prosperity, and the elephants are protected by laws. Receiving a gift of a white elephant could be both a blessing and curse as the animals cannot be put to practical use and are costly to care for.

WIN HANDS DOWN

To win easily, with little effort.

This phrase comes to us from the sport of horse racing. During competition a jockey has to hold the reins of the horse tight in order to encourage it run quickly. If a jockey has such a lead that he can lower his hands, and the reins of the horse, he is winning the race with great ease.

ON A WING AND A PRAYER

To chance it, to hope for the best and have faith, with perhaps only small chance of success.

The phrase comes from a Second World War song by Harold Adamson. He based his lyrics on the actual words spoken by the pilot of a damaged aircraft, who radioed the control tower as he prepared to come in to land. The 1943 song runs:

Tho' there's one motor gone, we can still carry on,
Comin' in on a wing and a pray'r.

Even in his moment of panic, the pilot might have been inspired by words from Psalm 104 (v.3):

Who layeth the beams of his chambers in the waters:
and maketh the clouds his chariot, and walketh upon the wings of the wind.

A WOLF IN SHEEP'S CLOTHING

Used to describe a malicious or dangerous person who uses a facade of innocence to fool others as to his or her true character.

The idea of such dissemblance has long been in circulation. One of the earliest phrases linking wolves and sheep comes from the Bible:

> Beware of false prophets, which come to you in sheep's clothing, but inwardly they are ravening wolves.
>
> Matthew 7:15

The original source of the phrase, however, is thought to be Aesop's fables, written in the sixth century BC. In the story, a wolf who is hunting sheep realizes that he can get close to the flock by disguising himself with a sheep's skin. But once he is among them, the shepherd—looking for a sheep to kill for his supper—mistakes the wolf for a suitable sheep and cuts its throat.

The moral of the story is that the wrongdoer will be punished by his own deceit.

WORTH ONE'S SALT

"Salt" is a significant euphemism, from the early nineteenth century onward, for one's financial worth, as a play on the word "salary," or the amount one earned.

In Roman times, a soldier received part of his pay in the form of a *salarium,* or salary, which was actually an allowance for the purchase of salt (the Latin for "salt" is *sal*). Salt was not easily obtainable then, and a soldier was not "worth his salt" if he did not **come up to scratch** (see page 52)—that is, did not deserve his *salarium.*

Consequently, to be "true to one's salt" is to be loyal to your employers, those who pay your salary, or to maintain or stand by one's personal honor.

THE WRITING ON THE WALL

This is not graffiti, but a bad sign, a portent, often foreshadowing trouble or disaster.

The metaphor is biblical in origin and comes from Daniel 5:5–31, where King Belshazzar, while he was feasting, found out about the forthcoming destruction of the Babylonian Empire through the mysterious appearance of handwriting on a wall.

The words read in Aramaic, *mene, mene, tekel, upharsin:* literally, "counted, weighed, divided." Daniel interpreted these words as, "You have been weighed in the balance and found wanting," thereby predicting the King's downfall and that of his empire.

Indeed, Belshazzar was killed that night, and his kingdom was conquered.

∾ Y ∾

YOU ARE WHAT YOU EAT

An informal slogan with "alternative-lifestyle" overtones that dates back to the 1960s. Today, the phrase is often associated with nutrition adviser Gillian McKeith's former popular TV show of the same name.

The idea behind the phrase, however, is far from new. In *Psychologie du Goût* (1825), the great philosopher of French cooking Anthelme Brillat-Savarin wrote, "Tell me what you eat and I will tell you what you are," while in 1945, the diarist Sir Henry "Chips" Channon fondly commented on the death of Sir Harcourt Johnstone, Liberal MP, bon vivant and Minister for Overseas Trade:

He dug his grave with his teeth.

YOU CAN'T MAKE A SILK PURSE OUT OF A SOW'S EAR

Don't attempt to make something good or of great value from what is naturally bad or inferior in quality. A similar old proverb is "you cannot make a horn out of a pig's ear."

To make a pig's ear of something is to botch it; the ear of a slaughtered pig being its most worthless part, no good for anything.

This ancient phrase was already a proverb by the mid 1500s and over time has inspired similar slang expressions, thought to have been instigated in the 1920s, such as "to make a dog's breakfast" or "dog's dinner" out of something.

YOU REAP WHAT YOU SOW

You cannot escape the consequences of your actions.

This agricultural metaphor expresses the idea that as a farmer reaps the harvest of the seeds he has sown in the earlier season, you face the repercussions of the actions you have taken. In other words, you get what you deserve. This maxim originates in the Biblical New Testament, in Paul's letters to the Galatians 6: 7-9:

> Be not deceived; God is not mocked: for whatsoever a man soweth, that shall he also reap. 8: For he that soweth to his flesh shall of the flesh reap corruption; but he that soweth to the Spirit shall of the Spirit reap life everlasting. 9: And let us not be weary in well doing: for in due season we shall reap, if we faint not.

~ Z ~

ZIP IT!

Be quiet!

This phrase is often used in exasperation when one is frustrated with what someone else is saying or perhaps complaining about. As you would close a bag by zipping it shut, you wish the whiny person would close his mouth and stop talking. This is similarly often expressed as, "Zip your lips!"

ZIGGED BEFORE YOU ZAGGED

You did things in the wrong order.

Perhaps used more for its assonance than any other reason, this playful phrase rolls off the tongue expressing that the actions you have taken may have been correct, but they were not in the correct order.

INDEX

Enjoy These Other Blackboard Books™

Anyone frightened by the subject of physics will learn that quantum mechanics doesn't bite—even if it does occasionally bang. Packed with amusing examples, this lively book distills all of the most important discoveries of physics.
$14.95 hardcover
ISBN 978–1–60652–171–7

Make learning fun again with these light-hearted pages that are packed with important theories, phrases, and those long-forgotten "rules" you once learned in school.
$14.95 hardcover
ISBN 978–0–7621–0995–1

What makes "seventh heaven" and "cloud nine" so blissful and the number 13 so unlucky? Why is "555" the fake area code of Hollywood? This delightful book explores the role of numbers in expressions, novels, film, cultures, religion, and more.

$14.95 hardcover
ISBN 978–1–60652–134–2

Confused about when to use "its" or "it's" or the correct spelling of "principal" or "principle"? Avoid language pitfalls and let this entertaining and practical guide improve both your speaking and writing skills.
$14.95 hardcover
ISBN 978–1–60652–026–0

A smorgasbord of foreign words and phrases used in everyday English—from Aficionado (Spanish) to Zeitgeist (German). Inside you'll find translations, definitions, and origins that will delight and amuse language lovers everywhere.
$14.95 hardcover
ISBN 978–1–60652–057–4

Reader's Digest books can be purchased through retail and online bookstores.
In the United States books are distributed by Penguin Group (USA), Inc.
For more information or to order books, call 1-800-788-6262.

Reader's
Digest